C-2812

THIS IS YOUR **PASSBOOK**® FOR ...

DIRECTOR OF MAINTENANCE

NATIONAL LEARNING CORPORATION®
passbooks.com

PASSBOOK® SERIES

THE *PASSBOOK® SERIES* has been created to prepare applicants and candidates for the ultimate academic battlefield – the examination room.

At some time in our lives, each and every one of us may be required to take an examination – for validation, matriculation, admission, qualification, registration, certification, or licensure.

Based on the assumption that every applicant or candidate has met the basic formal educational standards, has taken the required number of courses, and read the necessary texts, the *PASSBOOK® SERIES* furnishes the one special preparation which may assure passing with confidence, instead of failing with insecurity. Examination questions – together with answers – are furnished as the basic vehicle for study so that the mysteries of the examination and its compounding difficulties may be eliminated or diminished by a sure method.

This book is meant to help you pass your examination provided that you qualify and are serious in your objective.

The entire field is reviewed through the huge store of content information which is succinctly presented through a provocative and challenging approach – the question-and-answer method.

A climate of success is established by furnishing the correct answers at the end of each test.

You soon learn to recognize types of questions, forms of questions, and patterns of questioning. You may even begin to anticipate expected outcomes.

You perceive that many questions are repeated or adapted so that you can gain acute insights, which may enable you to score many sure points.

You learn how to confront new questions, or types of questions, and to attack them confidently and work out the correct answers.

You note objectives and emphases, and recognize pitfalls and dangers, so that you may make positive educational adjustments.

Moreover, you are kept fully informed in relation to new concepts, methods, practices, and directions in the field.

You discover that you arre actually taking the examination all the time: you are preparing for the examination by "taking" an examination, not by reading extraneous and/or supererogatory textbooks.

In short, this PASSBOOK®, used directedly, should be an important factor in helping you to pass your test.

DIRECTOR OF MAINTENANCE

DUTIES
Responsible for maintenance activities in a district, including facilities, stations, and collection systems; for the supervision and training of maintenance personnel assigned to various facilities and collection systems; also supervises the establishment and operation of a computerized maintenance record and scheduling program.

SCOPE OF THE WRITTEN TEST
The written test will be designed to cover knowledge, skills, and/or abilities in the following areas:
1. Inspection, operation, maintenance, and repair of basic mechanical equipment;
2. Operation, maintenance, and repair of pumps, motors, valves, mechanical and electrical equipment;
3. Practices and equipment used in plant operation and maintenance;
4. Hydraulic and pneumatic systems;
5. Work scheduling; and
6. Supervision.

HOW TO TAKE A TEST

I. YOU MUST PASS AN EXAMINATION

A. WHAT EVERY CANDIDATE SHOULD KNOW

Examination applicants often ask us for help in preparing for the written test. What can I study in advance? What kinds of questions will be asked? How will the test be given? How will the papers be graded?

As an applicant for a civil service examination, you may be wondering about some of these things. Our purpose here is to suggest effective methods of advance study and to describe civil service examinations.

Your chances for success on this examination can be increased if you know how to prepare. Those "pre-examination jitters" can be reduced if you know what to expect. You can even experience an adventure in good citizenship if you know why civil service exams are given.

B. WHY ARE CIVIL SERVICE EXAMINATIONS GIVEN?

Civil service examinations are important to you in two ways. As a citizen, you want public jobs filled by employees who know how to do their work. As a job seeker, you want a fair chance to compete for that job on an equal footing with other candidates. The best-known means of accomplishing this two-fold goal is the competitive examination.

Exams are widely publicized throughout the nation. They may be administered for jobs in federal, state, city, municipal, town or village governments or agencies.

Any citizen may apply, with some limitations, such as the age or residence of applicants. Your experience and education may be reviewed to see whether you meet the requirements for the particular examination. When these requirements exist, they are reasonable and applied consistently to all applicants. Thus, a competitive examination may cause you some uneasiness now, but it is your privilege and safeguard.

C. HOW ARE CIVIL SERVICE EXAMS DEVELOPED?

Examinations are carefully written by trained technicians who are specialists in the field known as "psychological measurement," in consultation with recognized authorities in the field of work that the test will cover. These experts recommend the subject matter areas or skills to be tested; only those knowledges or skills important to your success on the job are included. The most reliable books and source materials available are used as references. Together, the experts and technicians judge the difficulty level of the questions.

Test technicians know how to phrase questions so that the problem is clearly stated. Their ethics do not permit "trick" or "catch" questions. Questions may have been tried out on sample groups, or subjected to statistical analysis, to determine their usefulness.

Written tests are often used in combination with performance tests, ratings of training and experience, and oral interviews. All of these measures combine to form the best-known means of finding the right person for the right job.

II. HOW TO PASS THE WRITTEN TEST

A. *NATURE OF THE EXAMINATION*

To prepare intelligently for civil service examinations, you should know how they differ from school examinations you have taken. In school you were assigned certain definite pages to read or subjects to cover. The examination questions were quite detailed and usually emphasized memory. Civil service exams, on the other hand, try to discover your present ability to perform the duties of a position, plus your potentiality to learn these duties. In other words, a civil service exam attempts to predict how successful you will be. Questions cover such a broad area that they cannot be as minute and detailed as school exam questions.

In the public service similar kinds of work, or positions, are grouped together in one "class." This process is known as *position-classification*. All the positions in a class are paid according to the salary range for that class. One class title covers all of these positions, and they are all tested by the same examination.

B. *FOUR BASIC STEPS*

1) Study the announcement

How, then, can you know what subjects to study? Our best answer is: "Learn as much as possible about the class of positions for which you've applied." The exam will test the knowledge, skills and abilities needed to do the work.

Your most valuable source of information about the position you want is the official exam announcement. This announcement lists the training and experience qualifications. Check these standards and apply only if you come reasonably close to meeting them.

The brief description of the position in the examination announcement offers some clues to the subjects which will be tested. Think about the job itself. Review the duties in your mind. Can you perform them, or are there some in which you are rusty? Fill in the blank spots in your preparation.

Many jurisdictions preview the written test in the exam announcement by including a section called "Knowledge and Abilities Required," "Scope of the Examination," or some similar heading. Here you will find out specifically what fields will be tested.

2) Review your own background

Once you learn in general what the position is all about, and what you need to know to do the work, ask yourself which subjects you already know fairly well and which need improvement. You may wonder whether to concentrate on improving your strong areas or on building some background in your fields of weakness. When the announcement has specified "some knowledge" or "considerable knowledge," or has used adjectives like "beginning principles of..." or "advanced ... methods," you can get a clue as to the number and difficulty of questions to be asked in any given field. More questions, and hence broader coverage, would be included for those subjects which are more important in the work. Now weigh your strengths and weaknesses against the job requirements and prepare accordingly.

3) Determine the level of the position

Another way to tell how intensively you should prepare is to understand the level of the job for which you are applying. Is it the entering level? In other words, is this the position in which beginners in a field of work are hired? Or is it an intermediate or advanced level? Sometimes this is indicated by such words as "Junior" or "Senior" in the class title. Other jurisdictions use Roman numerals to designate the level – Clerk I, Clerk II, for example. The word "Supervisor" sometimes appears in the title. If the level is not indicated by the title, check the description of duties. Will you be working under very close supervision, or will you have responsibility for independent decisions in this work?

4) Choose appropriate study materials

Now that you know the subjects to be examined and the relative amount of each subject to be covered, you can choose suitable study materials. For beginning level jobs, or even advanced ones, if you have a pronounced weakness in some aspect of your training, read a modern, standard textbook in that field. Be sure it is up to date and has general coverage. Such books are normally available at your library, and the librarian will be glad to help you locate one. For entry-level positions, questions of appropriate difficulty are chosen – neither highly advanced questions, nor those too simple. Such questions require careful thought but not advanced training.

If the position for which you are applying is technical or advanced, you will read more advanced, specialized material. If you are already familiar with the basic principles of your field, elementary textbooks would waste your time. Concentrate on advanced textbooks and technical periodicals. Think through the concepts and review difficult problems in your field.

These are all general sources. You can get more ideas on your own initiative, following these leads. For example, training manuals and publications of the government agency which employs workers in your field can be useful, particularly for technical and professional positions. A letter or visit to the government department involved may result in more specific study suggestions, and certainly will provide you with a more definite idea of the exact nature of the position you are seeking.

III. KINDS OF TESTS

Tests are used for purposes other than measuring knowledge and ability to perform specified duties. For some positions, it is equally important to test ability to make adjustments to new situations or to profit from training. In others, basic mental abilities not dependent on information are essential. Questions which test these things may not appear as pertinent to the duties of the position as those which test for knowledge and information. Yet they are often highly important parts of a fair examination. For very general questions, it is almost impossible to help you direct your study efforts. What we can do is to point out some of the more common of these general abilities needed in public service positions and describe some typical questions.

1) General information

Broad, general information has been found useful for predicting job success in some kinds of work. This is tested in a variety of ways, from vocabulary lists to questions about current events. Basic background in some field of work, such as sociology or economics, may be sampled in a group of questions. Often these are principles which have become familiar to most persons through exposure rather than through formal training. It is difficult to advise you how to study for these questions; being alert to the world around you is our best suggestion.

2) Verbal ability

An example of an ability needed in many positions is verbal or language ability. Verbal ability is, in brief, the ability to use and understand words. Vocabulary and grammar tests are typical measures of this ability. Reading comprehension or paragraph interpretation questions are common in many kinds of civil service tests. You are given a paragraph of written material and asked to find its central meaning.

3) Numerical ability

Number skills can be tested by the familiar arithmetic problem, by checking paired lists of numbers to see which are alike and which are different, or by interpreting charts and graphs. In the latter test, a graph may be printed in the test booklet which you are asked to use as the basis for answering questions.

4) Observation

A popular test for law-enforcement positions is the observation test. A picture is shown to you for several minutes, then taken away. Questions about the picture test your ability to observe both details and larger elements.

5) Following directions

In many positions in the public service, the employee must be able to carry out written instructions dependably and accurately. You may be given a chart with several columns, each column listing a variety of information. The questions require you to carry out directions involving the information given in the chart.

6) Skills and aptitudes

Performance tests effectively measure some manual skills and aptitudes. When the skill is one in which you are trained, such as typing or shorthand, you can practice. These tests are often very much like those given in business school or high school courses. For many of the other skills and aptitudes, however, no short-time preparation can be made. Skills and abilities natural to you or that you have developed throughout your lifetime are being tested.

Many of the general questions just described provide all the data needed to answer the questions and ask you to use your reasoning ability to find the answers. Your best preparation for these tests, as well as for tests of facts and ideas, is to be at your physical and mental best. You, no doubt, have your own methods of getting into an exam-taking mood and keeping "in shape." The next section lists some ideas on this subject.

IV. KINDS OF QUESTIONS

Only rarely is the "essay" question, which you answer in narrative form, used in civil service tests. Civil service tests are usually of the short-answer type. Full instructions for answering these questions will be given to you at the examination. But in case this is your first experience with short-answer questions and separate answer sheets, here is what you need to know:

1) Multiple-choice Questions

Most popular of the short-answer questions is the "multiple choice" or "best answer" question. It can be used, for example, to test for factual knowledge, ability to solve problems or judgment in meeting situations found at work.

A multiple-choice question is normally one of three types—

- It can begin with an incomplete statement followed by several possible endings. You are to find the one ending which *best* completes the statement, although some of the others may not be entirely wrong.
- It can also be a complete statement in the form of a question which is answered by choosing one of the statements listed.
- It can be in the form of a problem – again you select the best answer.

Here is an example of a multiple-choice question with a discussion which should give you some clues as to the method for choosing the right answer:

When an employee has a complaint about his assignment, the action which will *best* help him overcome his difficulty is to
   A. discuss his difficulty with his coworkers
   B. take the problem to the head of the organization
   C. take the problem to the person who gave him the assignment
   D. say nothing to anyone about his complaint

In answering this question, you should study each of the choices to find which is best. Consider choice "A" – Certainly an employee may discuss his complaint with fellow employees, but no change or improvement can result, and the complaint remains unresolved. Choice "B" is a poor choice since the head of the organization probably does not know what assignment you have been given, and taking your problem to him is known as "going over the head" of the supervisor. The supervisor, or person who made the assignment, is the person who can clarify it or correct any injustice. Choice "C" is, therefore, correct. To say nothing, as in choice "D," is unwise. Supervisors have and interest in knowing the problems employees are facing, and the employee is seeking a solution to his problem.

2) True/False Questions

The "true/false" or "right/wrong" form of question is sometimes used. Here a complete statement is given. Your job is to decide whether the statement is right or wrong.

SAMPLE: A roaming cell-phone call to a nearby city costs less than a non-roaming call to a distant city.

This statement is wrong, or false, since roaming calls are more expensive.
This is not a complete list of all possible question forms, although most of the others are variations of these common types. You will always get complete directions for

answering questions. Be sure you understand *how* to mark your answers – ask questions until you do.

V. RECORDING YOUR ANSWERS

Computer terminals are used more and more today for many different kinds of exams.

For an examination with very few applicants, you may be told to record your answers in the test booklet itself. Separate answer sheets are much more common. If this separate answer sheet is to be scored by machine – and this is often the case – it is highly important that you mark your answers correctly in order to get credit.

An electronic scoring machine is often used in civil service offices because of the speed with which papers can be scored. Machine-scored answer sheets must be marked with a pencil, which will be given to you. This pencil has a high graphite content which responds to the electronic scoring machine. As a matter of fact, stray dots may register as answers, so do not let your pencil rest on the answer sheet while you are pondering the correct answer. Also, if your pencil lead breaks or is otherwise defective, ask for another.

Since the answer sheet will be dropped in a slot in the scoring machine, be careful not to bend the corners or get the paper crumpled.

The answer sheet normally has five vertical columns of numbers, with 30 numbers to a column. These numbers correspond to the question numbers in your test booklet. After each number, going across the page are four or five pairs of dotted lines. These short dotted lines have small letters or numbers above them. The first two pairs may also have a "T" or "F" above the letters. This indicates that the first two pairs only are to be used if the questions are of the true-false type. If the questions are multiple choice, disregard the "T" and "F" and pay attention only to the small letters or numbers.

Answer your questions in the manner of the sample that follows:

32. The largest city in the United States is
   A. Washington, D.C.
   B. New York City
   C. Chicago
   D. Detroit
   E. San Francisco

1) Choose the answer you think is best. (New York City is the largest, so "B" is correct.)
2) Find the row of dotted lines numbered the same as the question you are answering. (Find row number 32)
3) Find the pair of dotted lines corresponding to the answer. (Find the pair of lines under the mark "B.")
4) Make a solid black mark between the dotted lines.

VI. BEFORE THE TEST

Common sense will help you find procedures to follow to get ready for an examination. Too many of us, however, overlook these sensible measures. Indeed, nervousness and fatigue have been found to be the most serious reasons why applicants fail to do their best on civil service tests. Here is a list of reminders:

- Begin your preparation early – Don't wait until the last minute to go scurrying around for books and materials or to find out what the position is all about.
- Prepare continuously – An hour a night for a week is better than an all-night cram session. This has been definitely established. What is more, a night a week for a month will return better dividends than crowding your study into a shorter period of time.
- Locate the place of the exam – You have been sent a notice telling you when and where to report for the examination. If the location is in a different town or otherwise unfamiliar to you, it would be well to inquire the best route and learn something about the building.
- Relax the night before the test – Allow your mind to rest. Do not study at all that night. Plan some mild recreation or diversion; then go to bed early and get a good night's sleep.
- Get up early enough to make a leisurely trip to the place for the test – This way unforeseen events, traffic snarls, unfamiliar buildings, etc. will not upset you.
- Dress comfortably – A written test is not a fashion show. You will be known by number and not by name, so wear something comfortable.
- Leave excess paraphernalia at home – Shopping bags and odd bundles will get in your way. You need bring only the items mentioned in the official notice you received; usually everything you need is provided. Do not bring reference books to the exam. They will only confuse those last minutes and be taken away from you when in the test room.
- Arrive somewhat ahead of time – If because of transportation schedules you must get there very early, bring a newspaper or magazine to take your mind off yourself while waiting.
- Locate the examination room – When you have found the proper room, you will be directed to the seat or part of the room where you will sit. Sometimes you are given a sheet of instructions to read while you are waiting. Do not fill out any forms until you are told to do so; just read them and be prepared.
- Relax and prepare to listen to the instructions
- If you have any physical problem that may keep you from doing your best, be sure to tell the test administrator. If you are sick or in poor health, you really cannot do your best on the exam. You can come back and take the test some other time.

VII. AT THE TEST

The day of the test is here and you have the test booklet in your hand. The temptation to get going is very strong. Caution! There is more to success than knowing the right answers. You must know how to identify your papers and understand variations in the type of short-answer question used in this particular examination. Follow these suggestions for maximum results from your efforts:

1) Cooperate with the monitor

The test administrator has a duty to create a situation in which you can be as much at ease as possible. He will give instructions, tell you when to begin, check to see that you are marking your answer sheet correctly, and so on. He is not there to guard you, although he will see that your competitors do not take unfair advantage. He wants to help you do your best.

2) Listen to all instructions

Don't jump the gun! Wait until you understand all directions. In most civil service tests you get more time than you need to answer the questions. So don't be in a hurry. Read each word of instructions until you clearly understand the meaning. Study the examples, listen to all announcements and follow directions. Ask questions if you do not understand what to do.

3) Identify your papers

Civil service exams are usually identified by number only. You will be assigned a number; you must not put your name on your test papers. Be sure to copy your number correctly. Since more than one exam may be given, copy your exact examination title.

4) Plan your time

Unless you are told that a test is a "speed" or "rate of work" test, speed itself is usually not important. Time enough to answer all the questions will be provided, but this does not mean that you have all day. An overall time limit has been set. Divide the total time (in minutes) by the number of questions to determine the approximate time you have for each question.

5) Do not linger over difficult questions

If you come across a difficult question, mark it with a paper clip (useful to have along) and come back to it when you have been through the booklet. One caution if you do this – be sure to skip a number on your answer sheet as well. Check often to be sure that you have not lost your place and that you are marking in the row numbered the same as the question you are answering.

6) Read the questions

Be sure you know what the question asks! Many capable people are unsuccessful because they failed to *read* the questions correctly.

7) Answer all questions

Unless you have been instructed that a penalty will be deducted for incorrect answers, it is better to guess than to omit a question.

8) Speed tests

It is often better NOT to guess on speed tests. It has been found that on timed tests people are tempted to spend the last few seconds before time is called in marking answers at random – without even reading them – in the hope of picking up a few extra points. To discourage this practice, the instructions may warn you that your score will be "corrected" for guessing. That is, a penalty will be applied. The incorrect answers will be deducted from the correct ones, or some other penalty formula will be used.

9) Review your answers

If you finish before time is called, go back to the questions you guessed or omitted to give them further thought. Review other answers if you have time.

10) Return your test materials

If you are ready to leave before others have finished or time is called, take ALL your materials to the monitor and leave quietly. Never take any test material with you. The monitor can discover whose papers are not complete, and taking a test booklet may be grounds for disqualification.

VIII. EXAMINATION TECHNIQUES

1) Read the general instructions carefully. These are usually printed on the first page of the exam booklet. As a rule, these instructions refer to the timing of the examination; the fact that you should not start work until the signal and must stop work at a signal, etc. If there are any *special* instructions, such as a choice of questions to be answered, make sure that you note this instruction carefully.

2) When you are ready to start work on the examination, that is as soon as the signal has been given, read the instructions to each question booklet, underline any key words or phrases, such as *least, best, outline, describe* and the like. In this way you will tend to answer as requested rather than discover on reviewing your paper that you *listed without describing*, that you selected the *worst* choice rather than the *best* choice, etc.

3) If the examination is of the objective or multiple-choice type – that is, each question will also give a series of possible answers: A, B, C or D, and you are called upon to select the best answer and write the letter next to that answer on your answer paper – it is advisable to start answering each question in turn. There may be anywhere from 50 to 100 such questions in the three or four hours allotted and you can see how much time would be taken if you read through all the questions before beginning to answer any. Furthermore, if you come across a question or group of questions which you know would be difficult to answer, it would undoubtedly affect your handling of all the other questions.

4) If the examination is of the essay type and contains but a few questions, it is a moot point as to whether you should read all the questions before starting to answer any one. Of course, if you are given a choice – say five out of seven and the like – then it is essential to read all the questions so you can eliminate the two that are most difficult. If, however, you are asked to answer all the questions, there may be danger in trying to answer the easiest one first because you may find that you will spend too much time on it. The best technique is to answer the first question, then proceed to the second, etc.

5) Time your answers. Before the exam begins, write down the time it started, then add the time allowed for the examination and write down the time it must be completed, then divide the time available somewhat as follows:

- If 3-1/2 hours are allowed, that would be 210 minutes. If you have 80 objective-type questions, that would be an average of 2-1/2 minutes per question. Allow yourself no more than 2 minutes per question, or a total of 160 minutes, which will permit about 50 minutes to review.
- If for the time allotment of 210 minutes there are 7 essay questions to answer, that would average about 30 minutes a question. Give yourself only 25 minutes per question so that you have about 35 minutes to review.

6) The most important instruction is to *read each question* and make sure you know what is wanted. The second most important instruction is to *time yourself properly* so that you answer every question. The third most important instruction is to *answer every question*. Guess if you have to but include something for each question. Remember that you will receive no credit for a blank and will probably receive some credit if you write something in answer to an essay question. If you guess a letter – say "B" for a multiple-choice question – you may have guessed right. If you leave a blank as an answer to a multiple-choice question, the examiners may respect your feelings but it will not add a point to your score. Some exams may penalize you for wrong answers, so in such cases *only*, you may not want to guess unless you have some basis for your answer.

7) Suggestions
   a. Objective-type questions
      1. Examine the question booklet for proper sequence of pages and questions
      2. Read all instructions carefully
      3. Skip any question which seems too difficult; return to it after all other questions have been answered
      4. Apportion your time properly; do not spend too much time on any single question or group of questions
      5. Note and underline key words – *all, most, fewest, least, best, worst, same, opposite,* etc.
      6. Pay particular attention to negatives
      7. Note unusual option, e.g., unduly long, short, complex, different or similar in content to the body of the question
      8. Observe the use of "hedging" words – *probably, may, most likely,* etc.
      9. Make sure that your answer is put next to the same number as the question
      10. Do not second-guess unless you have good reason to believe the second answer is definitely more correct
      11. Cross out original answer if you decide another answer is more accurate; do not erase until you are ready to hand your paper in
      12. Answer all questions; guess unless instructed otherwise
      13. Leave time for review

   b. Essay questions
      1. Read each question carefully
      2. Determine exactly what is wanted. Underline key words or phrases.
      3. Decide on outline or paragraph answer

4. Include many different points and elements unless asked to develop any one or two points or elements
5. Show impartiality by giving pros and cons unless directed to select one side only
6. Make and write down any assumptions you find necessary to answer the questions
7. Watch your English, grammar, punctuation and choice of words
8. Time your answers; don't crowd material

8) Answering the essay question

Most essay questions can be answered by framing the specific response around several key words or ideas. Here are a few such key words or ideas:

M's: manpower, materials, methods, money, management
P's: purpose, program, policy, plan, procedure, practice, problems, pitfalls, personnel, public relations
   a. Six basic steps in handling problems:
      1. Preliminary plan and background development
      2. Collect information, data and facts
      3. Analyze and interpret information, data and facts
      4. Analyze and develop solutions as well as make recommendations
      5. Prepare report and sell recommendations
      6. Install recommendations and follow up effectiveness

   b. Pitfalls to avoid
      1. *Taking things for granted* – A statement of the situation does not necessarily imply that each of the elements is necessarily true; for example, a complaint may be invalid and biased so that all that can be taken for granted is that a complaint has been registered
      2. *Considering only one side of a situation* – Wherever possible, indicate several alternatives and then point out the reasons you selected the best one
      3. *Failing to indicate follow up* – Whenever your answer indicates action on your part, make certain that you will take proper follow-up action to see how successful your recommendations, procedures or actions turn out to be
      4. *Taking too long in answering any single question* – Remember to time your answers properly

IX. AFTER THE TEST

Scoring procedures differ in detail among civil service jurisdictions although the general principles are the same. Whether the papers are hand-scored or graded by machine we have described, they are nearly always graded by number. That is, the person who marks the paper knows only the number – never the name – of the applicant. Not until all the papers have been graded will they be matched with names. If other tests, such as training and experience or oral interview ratings have been given, scores will be combined. Different parts of the examination usually have different weights. For example, the written test might count 60 percent of the final grade, and a rating of training and experience 40 percent. In many jurisdictions, veterans will have a certain number of points added to their grades.

After the final grade has been determined, the names are placed in grade order and an eligible list is established. There are various methods for resolving ties between those who get the same final grade – probably the most common is to place first the name of the person whose application was received first. Job offers are made from the eligible list in the order the names appear on it. You will be notified of your grade and your rank as soon as all these computations have been made. This will be done as rapidly as possible.

People who are found to meet the requirements in the announcement are called "eligibles." Their names are put on a list of eligible candidates. An eligible's chances of getting a job depend on how high he stands on this list and how fast agencies are filling jobs from the list.

When a job is to be filled from a list of eligibles, the agency asks for the names of people on the list of eligibles for that job. When the civil service commission receives this request, it sends to the agency the names of the three people highest on this list. Or, if the job to be filled has specialized requirements, the office sends the agency the names of the top three persons who meet these requirements from the general list.

The appointing officer makes a choice from among the three people whose names were sent to him. If the selected person accepts the appointment, the names of the others are put back on the list to be considered for future openings.

That is the rule in hiring from all kinds of eligible lists, whether they are for typist, carpenter, chemist, or something else. For every vacancy, the appointing officer has his choice of any one of the top three eligibles on the list. This explains why the person whose name is on top of the list sometimes does not get an appointment when some of the persons lower on the list do. If the appointing officer chooses the second or third eligible, the No. 1 eligible does not get a job at once, but stays on the list until he is appointed or the list is terminated.

X. HOW TO PASS THE INTERVIEW TEST

The examination for which you applied requires an oral interview test. You have already taken the written test and you are now being called for the interview test – the final part of the formal examination.

You may think that it is not possible to prepare for an interview test and that there are no procedures to follow during an interview. Our purpose is to point out some things you can do in advance that will help you and some good rules to follow and pitfalls to avoid while you are being interviewed.

What is an interview supposed to test?

The written examination is designed to test the technical knowledge and competence of the candidate; the oral is designed to evaluate intangible qualities, not readily measured otherwise, and to establish a list showing the relative fitness of each candidate – as measured against his competitors – for the position sought. Scoring is not on the basis of "right" and "wrong," but on a sliding scale of values ranging from "not passable" to "outstanding." As a matter of fact, it is possible to achieve a relatively low score without a single "incorrect" answer because of evident weakness in the qualities being measured.

Occasionally, an examination may consist entirely of an oral test – either an individual or a group oral. In such cases, information is sought concerning the technical knowledges and abilities of the candidate, since there has been no written examination for this purpose. More commonly, however, an oral test is used to supplement a written examination.

Who conducts interviews?

The composition of oral boards varies among different jurisdictions. In nearly all, a representative of the personnel department serves as chairman. One of the members of the board may be a representative of the department in which the candidate would work. In some cases, "outside experts" are used, and, frequently, a businessman or some other representative of the general public is asked to serve. Labor and management or other special groups may be represented. The aim is to secure the services of experts in the appropriate field.

However the board is composed, it is a good idea (and not at all improper or unethical) to ascertain in advance of the interview who the members are and what groups they represent. When you are introduced to them, you will have some idea of their backgrounds and interests, and at least you will not stutter and stammer over their names.

What should be done before the interview?

While knowledge about the board members is useful and takes some of the surprise element out of the interview, there is other preparation which is more substantive. It *is* possible to prepare for an oral interview – in several ways:

1) Keep a copy of your application and review it carefully before the interview

This may be the only document before the oral board, and the starting point of the interview. Know what education and experience you have listed there, and the sequence and dates of all of it. Sometimes the board will ask you to review the highlights of your experience for them; you should not have to hem and haw doing it.

2) Study the class specification and the examination announcement

Usually, the oral board has one or both of these to guide them. The qualities, characteristics or knowledges required by the position sought are stated in these documents. They offer valuable clues as to the nature of the oral interview. For example, if the job involves supervisory responsibilities, the announcement will usually indicate that knowledge of modern supervisory methods and the qualifications of the candidate as a supervisor will be tested. If so, you can expect such questions, frequently in the form of a hypothetical situation which you are expected to solve. NEVER go into an oral without knowledge of the duties and responsibilities of the job you seek.

3) Think through each qualification required

Try to visualize the kind of questions you would ask if you were a board member. How well could you answer them? Try especially to appraise your own knowledge and background in each area, *measured against the job sought*, and identify any areas in which you are weak. Be critical and realistic – do not flatter yourself.

4) Do some general reading in areas in which you feel you may be weak

For example, if the job involves supervision and your past experience has NOT, some general reading in supervisory methods and practices, particularly in the field of human relations, might be useful. Do NOT study agency procedures or detailed manuals. The oral board will be testing your understanding and capacity, not your memory.

5) Get a good night's sleep and watch your general health and mental attitude

You will want a clear head at the interview. Take care of a cold or any other minor ailment, and of course, no hangovers.

What should be done on the day of the interview?

Now comes the day of the interview itself. Give yourself plenty of time to get there. Plan to arrive somewhat ahead of the scheduled time, particularly if your appointment is in the fore part of the day. If a previous candidate fails to appear, the board might be ready for you a bit early. By early afternoon an oral board is almost invariably behind schedule if there are many candidates, and you may have to wait. Take along a book or magazine to read, or your application to review, but leave any extraneous material in the waiting room when you go in for your interview. In any event, relax and compose yourself.

The matter of dress is important. The board is forming impressions about you – from your experience, your manners, your attitude, and your appearance. Give your personal appearance careful attention. Dress your best, but not your flashiest. Choose conservative, appropriate clothing, and be sure it is immaculate. This is a business interview, and your appearance should indicate that you regard it as such. Besides, being well groomed and properly dressed will help boost your confidence.

Sooner or later, someone will call your name and escort you into the interview room. *This is it.* From here on you are on your own. It is too late for any more preparation. But remember, you asked for this opportunity to prove your fitness, and you are here because your request was granted.

What happens when you go in?

The usual sequence of events will be as follows: The clerk (who is often the board stenographer) will introduce you to the chairman of the oral board, who will introduce you to the other members of the board. Acknowledge the introductions before you sit down. Do not be surprised if you find a microphone facing you or a stenotypist sitting by. Oral interviews are usually recorded in the event of an appeal or other review.

Usually the chairman of the board will open the interview by reviewing the highlights of your education and work experience from your application – primarily for the benefit of the other members of the board, as well as to get the material into the record. Do not interrupt or comment unless there is an error or significant misinterpretation; if that is the case, do not hesitate. But do not quibble about insignificant matters. Also, he will usually ask you some question about your education, experience or your present job – partly to get you to start talking and to establish the interviewing "rapport." He may start the actual questioning, or turn it over to one of the other members. Frequently, each member undertakes the questioning on a particular area, one in which he is perhaps most competent, so you can expect each member to participate in the examination. Because time is limited, you may also expect some rather abrupt switches in the direction the questioning takes, so do not be upset by it. Normally, a board member will not pursue a single line of questioning unless he discovers a particular strength or weakness.

After each member has participated, the chairman will usually ask whether any member has any further questions, then will ask you if you have anything you wish to add. Unless you are expecting this question, it may floor you. Worse, it may start you off on an extended, extemporaneous speech. The board is not usually seeking more information. The question is principally to offer you a last opportunity to present further qualifications or to indicate that you have nothing to add. So, if you feel that a significant qualification or characteristic has been overlooked, it is proper to point it out in a sentence or so. Do not compliment the board on the thoroughness of their examination – they have been sketchy, and you know it. If you wish, merely say, "No thank you, I have nothing further to add." This is a point where you can "talk yourself out" of a good impression or fail to present an important bit of information. Remember, *you close the interview yourself.*

The chairman will then say, "That is all, Mr. _____, thank you." Do not be startled; the interview is over, and quicker than you think. Thank him, gather your belongings and take your leave. Save your sigh of relief for the other side of the door.

How to put your best foot forward

Throughout this entire process, you may feel that the board individually and collectively is trying to pierce your defenses, seek out your hidden weaknesses and embarrass and confuse you. Actually, this is not true. They are obliged to make an appraisal of your qualifications for the job you are seeking, and they want to see you in your best light. Remember, they must interview all candidates and a non-cooperative candidate may become a failure in spite of their best efforts to bring out his qualifications. Here are 15 suggestions that will help you:

1) Be natural – Keep your attitude confident, not cocky

If you are not confident that you can do the job, do not expect the board to be. Do not apologize for your weaknesses, try to bring out your strong points. The board is interested in a positive, not negative, presentation. Cockiness will antagonize any board member and make him wonder if you are covering up a weakness by a false show of strength.

2) Get comfortable, but don't lounge or sprawl

Sit erectly but not stiffly. A careless posture may lead the board to conclude that you are careless in other things, or at least that you are not impressed by the importance of the occasion. Either conclusion is natural, even if incorrect. Do not fuss with your clothing, a pencil or an ashtray. Your hands may occasionally be useful to emphasize a point; do not let them become a point of distraction.

3) Do not wisecrack or make small talk

This is a serious situation, and your attitude should show that you consider it as such. Further, the time of the board is limited – they do not want to waste it, and neither should you.

4) Do not exaggerate your experience or abilities

In the first place, from information in the application or other interviews and sources, the board may know more about you than you think. Secondly, you probably will not get away with it. An experienced board is rather adept at spotting such a situation, so do not take the chance.

5) If you know a board member, do not make a point of it, yet do not hide it

Certainly you are not fooling him, and probably not the other members of the board. Do not try to take advantage of your acquaintanceship – it will probably do you little good.

6) Do not dominate the interview

Let the board do that. They will give you the clues – do not assume that you have to do all the talking. Realize that the board has a number of questions to ask you, and do not try to take up all the interview time by showing off your extensive knowledge of the answer to the first one.

7) Be attentive

You only have 20 minutes or so, and you should keep your attention at its sharpest throughout. When a member is addressing a problem or question to you, give him your undivided attention. Address your reply principally to him, but do not exclude the other board members.

8) Do not interrupt

A board member may be stating a problem for you to analyze. He will ask you a question when the time comes. Let him state the problem, and wait for the question.

9) Make sure you understand the question

Do not try to answer until you are sure what the question is. If it is not clear, restate it in your own words or ask the board member to clarify it for you. However, do not haggle about minor elements.

10) Reply promptly but not hastily

A common entry on oral board rating sheets is "candidate responded readily," or "candidate hesitated in replies." Respond as promptly and quickly as you can, but do not jump to a hasty, ill-considered answer.

11) Do not be peremptory in your answers

A brief answer is proper – but do not fire your answer back. That is a losing game from your point of view. The board member can probably ask questions much faster than you can answer them.

12) Do not try to create the answer you think the board member wants

He is interested in what kind of mind you have and how it works – not in playing games. Furthermore, he can usually spot this practice and will actually grade you down on it.

13) Do not switch sides in your reply merely to agree with a board member

Frequently, a member will take a contrary position merely to draw you out and to see if you are willing and able to defend your point of view. Do not start a debate, yet do not surrender a good position. If a position is worth taking, it is worth defending.

14) Do not be afraid to admit an error in judgment if you are shown to be wrong

The board knows that you are forced to reply without any opportunity for careful consideration. Your answer may be demonstrably wrong. If so, admit it and get on with the interview.

15) Do not dwell at length on your present job

The opening question may relate to your present assignment. Answer the question but do not go into an extended discussion. You are being examined for a *new* job, not your present one. As a matter of fact, try to phrase ALL your answers in terms of the job for which you are being examined.

Basis of Rating

Probably you will forget most of these "do's" and "don'ts" when you walk into the oral interview room. Even remembering them all will not ensure you a passing grade. Perhaps you did not have the qualifications in the first place. But remembering them will help you to put your best foot forward, without treading on the toes of the board members.

Rumor and popular opinion to the contrary notwithstanding, an oral board wants you to make the best appearance possible. They know you are under pressure – but they also want to see how you respond to it as a guide to what your reaction would be under the pressures of the job you seek. They will be influenced by the degree of poise you display, the personal traits you show and the manner in which you respond.

ABOUT THIS BOOK

This book contains tests divided into Examination Sections. Go through each test, answering every question in the margin. At the end of each test look at the answer key and check your answers. On the ones you got wrong, look at the right answer choice and learn. Do not fill in the answers first. Do not memorize the questions and answers, but understand the answer and principles involved. On your test, the questions will likely be different from the samples. Questions are changed and new ones added. If you understand these past questions you should have success with any changes that arise. Tests may consist of several types of questions. We have additional books on each subject should more study be advisable or necessary for you. Finally, the more you study, the better prepared you will be. This book is intended to be the last thing you study before you walk into the examination room. Prior study of relevant texts is also recommended. NLC publishes some of these in our Fundamental Series. Knowledge and good sense are important factors in passing your exam. Good luck also helps. So now study this Passbook, absorb the material contained within and take that knowledge into the examination. Then do your best to pass that exam.

EXAMINATION SECTION

EXAMINATION SECTION
TEST 1

DIRECTIONS: Each question or incomplete statement is followed by several suggested answers or completions. Select the one that BEST answers the question or completes the statement. *PRINT THE LETTER OF THE CORRECT ANSWER IN THE SPACE AT THE RIGHT.*

Questions 1-3.

DIRECTIONS: Questions 1 through 3, inclusive, are to be answered in accordance with the American Standard Graphical Symbols for Pipe Fittings, Valves, and Piping and American Standard Graphical Symbols for Heating, Ventilating and Air Conditioning.

1. The symbol ⊙—|—— shown on a piping drawing represents a _____ elbow.   1._____

    A. turned down   B. reducing
    C. long radius   D. turned up

2. The symbol ——▭—— shown on a heating drawing represents a(n)   2._____

    A. expansion joint   B. hanger or support
    C. heat exchanger   D. air eliminator

3._____

3. The symbol ——|◄►|—— shown on a piping drawing represents a _____ gate valve.

    A. welded   B. flanged
    C. screwed   D. bell and spigot

4. The MAIN purpose for the inspection of plant equipment, buildings, and facilities is to   4._____

    A. determine the quality of maintenance work of all the trades
    B. prevent the overstocking of equipment and materials used in maintenance work
    C. forecast normal maintenance jobs for existing equipment, buildings, and facilities
    D. prevent unscheduled interruptions of operating equipment and excessive deterioration of buildings and facilities

5. Of the following devices, the one that is used to determine the rating, in cubic feet per minute, of a unit ventilator is a(n)   5._____

    A. psychrometer   B. pyrometer
    C. anemometer   D. manometer

6. A number of 4' x 6' skids loaded with material are to be stored. Assume that the total weight of each loaded skid is 1200 pounds and that the maximum allowable floor load is 280 lbs. per sq. ft.
The MAXIMUM number of skids that can be stacked vertically without exceeding the MAXIMUM allowable floor load is   6._____

    A. 4   B. 5   C. 6   D. 7

7. Specifications which contain the term *slump test* would MOST likely refer to   7._____

   A. lumber   B. paint   C. concrete   D. water

8. Of the following sizes of copper conductors, the one which has the LEAST current-carry-   8._____
   ing capacity is _____ AWG.

   A. 000   B. 0   C. 8   D. 12

9. The size of a steel beam is shown on a steel drawing as W 8 x 15.   9._____
   In accordance with the latest edition of the Steel Construction Manual of the American
   Institute of Steel Construction, the number 8 in W 8 x 15 represents the beam's
   approximate

   A. depth   B. flange thickness
   C. width   D. web thickness

10. For expediting control functions such as work methods, planning, scheduling, and work   10._____
    measurement, EQUIPMENT RECORDS must contain specific data.
    Of the following, the data which is NOT usually indicated on an EQUIPMENT
    RECORD card is

    A. machinery and parts specifications numbers
    B. a breakdown history
    C. a preventive maintenance history
    D. salvage value on the open market

11. Refrigeration piping, valves, fittings, and related parts used in the construction and instal-   11._____
    lation of refrigeration systems shall conform to the

    A. American Society of Mechanical Engineers Boiler and Pressure Vessel Code
    B. American Standards Association Code for Pressure Piping
    C. Pipe Fabrication Institute Standards
    D. Underwriters Laboratory Standards

12. The maintenance term *downtime* means MOST NEARLY the   12._____

    A. period of time in which a machine is out of service
    B. routine replacement of parts or materials to a piece of equipment
    C. labor required for clean-up of equipment to insure its proper operation
    D. maintenance work which is confined to checking, adjusting, and lubrication of
       equipment

13. A supplier quotes a list price of $172.00 less 15 and 10 percent for twelve tools.   13._____
    The ACTUAL cost for these twelve tools is MOST NEARLY

    A. $146   B. $132   C. $129   D. $112

14. Of the following colors of electrical conductor coverings, the one which indicates a con-   14._____
    ductor used SOLELY for grounding portable or fixed electrical equipment is

    A. blue   B. green   C. red   D. black

15. A *medium duty* type of scaffold is one on which the working load on the platform surface   15._____
    must NOT exceed _____ pounds per square foot.

    A. 50   B. 70   C. 90   D. 110

16. Assume that a mechanic is using a powder-actuated tool and the cartridge misfires. According to recommended safe practices regarding a misfired cartridge, the FIRST course of action the mechanic should take is to   16._____

    A. place the misfired cartridge carefully into a metal container filled with water
    B. carefully reload the tool with the misfired cartridge and try it again
    C. immediately bury the misfired cartridge at least two feet in the ground
    D. remove the wadding from the misfired cartridge and empty the powder into a pail of sand

17. The ratings used in classifying fire resistant building construction materials are MOST frequently expressed in   17._____

    A. Btu's   B. hours   C. temperatures   D. pounds

18. The only legible portion of the nameplate on a piece of equipment reads: *208 volts, 3 phase, 10 H.P.*
This data would MOST NEARLY indicate that the piece of equipment is a(n)   18._____

    A. amplifier   B. fixture ballast
    C. motor   D. rectifier

19. Of the following items relating to the maintenance of roofs, the one which is of the LEAST value in a preventive maintenance program for roofs is knowledge of the   19._____

    A. roofing specifications   B. application procedures
    C. process of deterioration   D. frequency of rainstorms

20. In an oxyacetylene cutting outfit, the color of the hose that is connected to the oxygen cylinder is USUALLY   20._____

    A. white   B. yellow   C. red   D. green

21. Assume that a welding generator is to be used to weld partitions made of 18 gauge steel. Of the following settings, the BEST one to use would be a _____ setting of voltage and a _____ setting of amperage.   21._____

    A. high; high   B. high; low   C. low; high   D. low; low

22. According to the administrative code, when color marking is used, potable water lines shall be painted   22._____

    A. yellow   B. blue   C. red   D. green

23. A set of mechanical plan drawings is drawn to a scale of 1/8" = 1 foot.
If a length of pipe measures 15 7/16" on the drawing, the ACTUAL length of the pipe is _____ feet.   23._____

    A. 121.5   B. 122.5   C. 123.5   D. 124.5

24. A portion of a specification states: *Concrete, other than that placed under water, should be compacted and worked into place by spading or puddling.*
The MAIN reason why *spading and puddling* is required is to   24._____

    A. insure that all water in the concrete mix is brought to the surface
    B. eliminate stone pockets and large bubbles of air

4 (#1)

C. provide a means to obtain a spade full of concrete for test purposes
D. make allowances for *bleeding and segregation* of the concrete

25. Assume that the following statement appears in a construction contract: *Payment will be made for the number of pounds of bar reinforcement incorporated in the work as shown on the plans.*
This type of contract is MOST likely   25.____

    A. cost plus   B. lump sum   C. subcontract   D. unit price

26. Partial payments to outside contractors are USUALLY based on the   26.____

    A. breakdown estimate submitted after the contract was signed
    B. actual cost of labor and material plus overhead and profit
    C. estimate of work completed which is generally submitted periodically
    D. estimate of material delivered to the job

27. Building contracts usually require that estimates for changes made in the field be submitted for approval before the work can start.   27.____
The MAIN reason for this requirement is to

    A. make sure that the contractor understands the change
    B. discourage such changes
    C. keep the contractor honest
    D. enable the department to control its expenses

28. An *addendum* to contract specifications means MOST NEARLY   28.____

    A. a substantial completion payment to the contractor for work almost completed
    B. final acceptance of the work by authorities of all contract work still to be done
    C. additional contract provisions issued in writing by authorities prior to receipt of bids
    D. work other than that required by the contract at the time of its execution

29. Of the following terms, the one which is usually NOT used to describe the types of payments to outside contractors for work done is the _____ payment.   29.____

    A. partial payment   B. substantial completion
    C. final   D. surety

30. Of the following metals, the one which is a ferrous metal is   30.____

    A. cast iron   B. brass   C. bronze   D. babbit

31. Assume that you have assigned six mechanics to do a job that must be finished in four days. At the end of three days, your men have completed only two-thirds of the job. In order to complete the job on time and because the job is such that it cannot be speeded up, you should assign a MINIMUM of _____ extra men.   31.____

    A. 3   B. 4   C. 5   D. 6

32. Of the following traps, the one which is NORMALLY used to retain steam in a heating unit or piping is the _____ trap.   32.____

    A. P   B. running   C. float   D. bell

4

33. Of the following materials, the one which is a convenient and powerful adhesive for cementing tears in canvas jackets that are wrapped around warm pipe insulation is   33.____

    A. cylinder oil   B. wheat paste
    C. water glass   D. latex paint

34. Pipe chases should be provided with an access door PRIMARILY to provide means to   34.____

    A. replace piping lines
    B. either inspect or manipulate valves
    C. prevent condensate from forming on the pipes
    D. check the chase for possible structural defects

35. Electric power is measured in   35.____

    A. volts   B. amperes   C. watts   D. ohms

KEY (CORRECT ANSWERS)

1.	D		16.	A
2.	A		17.	B
3.	B		18.	C
4.	D		19.	D
5.	C		20.	D
6.	B		21.	B
7.	C		22.	D
8.	D		23.	C
9.	A		24.	B
10.	D		25.	D
11.	B		26.	C
12.	A		27.	D
13.	B		28.	C
14.	B		29.	D
15.	A		30.	A

31.	A
32.	C
33.	C
34.	B
35.	C

TEST 2

DIRECTIONS: Each question or incomplete statement is followed by several suggested answers or completions. Select the one that BEST answers the question or completes the statement. *PRINT THE LETTER OF THE CORRECT ANSWER IN THE SPACE AT THE RIGHT.*

1. The HIGHEST quality tools should   1._____

    A. always be bought
    B. never be bought
    C. be bought when they offer an overall advantage
    D. be bought only for foreman

2. Master keys should have no markings that will identify them as such.   2._____
    This statement is

    A. *false;* it would be impossible to keep records about them without such markings
    B. *true;* markings are subject to alteration and vandalization
    C. *false;* without such markings, they would be too lightly regarded by those to whom issued
    D. *true;* markings would only highlight their value to a potential wrongdoer

3. For a foreman to usually delay for a few weeks handling grievances his men make is a   3._____

    A. *poor* practice; it can affect the morale of the men
    B. *good* practice; it will discourage grievances
    C. *poor* practice; the causes of grievances usually disappear if action is delayed
    D. *good* practice; most employee grievances are not justified

4. Whenever an important change in procedure is contemplated, some foremen make a   4._____
    point of discussing the matter with their subordinates in order to get their viewpoint on
    the proposed change.
    In general, this practice is advisable MAINLY for the reason that

    A. subordinates can often see the effects of procedural changes more clearly than foremen
    B. the foreman has an opportunity to explain the advantages of the new procedure
    C. future changes will be welcomed if subordinates are kept informed
    D. participation in work planning helps to build a spirit of cooperation among employees

5. An estimate of employee morale could LEAST effectively be appraised by   5._____

    A. checking accident and absenteeism records
    B. determining the attitudes of employees toward their job
    C. examining the number of requests for emergency leaves of absence
    D. reviewing the number and nature of employee suggestions

6. Assume that you are a foreman and that a visitor at the job site asks you what your crew   6._____
    is doing.
    You should

A. respectfully decline to answer since all questions must be answered by the proper authority
B. answer as concisely as possible but discourage undue conversation
C. refer the man to your superiors
D. give the person complete details of the job

7. Cooperation can BEST be obtained from the general public by   7.____

   A. siding with them whenever they have a complaint
   B. sticking carefully to your work and ignoring everything else
   C. explaining the department's objectives and why the public must occasionally be temporarily inconvenienced
   D. listening politely to their complaints and telling them that the complaints will be forwarded to the main office

8. While you are working for the city, a man says to you that one of the rules of your job   8.____
   doesn't make sense and he gets mad.
   You should say to him

   A. Leave me alone so I can get my work done
   B. Everyone must follow the rules
   C. Let me tell you the reason for the rule
   D. I'm only doing my job so don't get mad at me

9. One approach to preparing written reports to superiors is to present first the conclusions   9.____
   and recommendations and then the data on which the conclusions and recommendations are based.
   The use of this approach is BEST justified when the

   A. data completely support the conclusions and recommendations
   B. superiors lack the specific training and experience required to understand and interpret the data
   C. data contain more information than is required for making the conclusions and recommendations
   D. superiors are more interested in the conclusions and recommendations than in the data

10. The MOST important reason why separate paragraphs might be used in writing a report   10.____
    is that this

    A. makes it easier to understand the report
    B. permits the report to be condensed
    C. gives a better appearance to the report
    D. prevents accidental elimination of important facts

11. On a drawing, the following standard cross-section represents MOST NEARLY   11.____

    A. sand   B. concrete   C. earth   D. rock

12. On a drawing, the following standard cross-section represents MOST NEARLY 　　　　12.____

    A. malleable iron   B. steel
    C. bronze   D. lead

13. On a piping plan drawing, the symbol represents a 90° _____ elbow. 　　　　13.____

    A. flanged   B. screwed
    C. bell and spigot   D. welded

14. On a drawing, the symbol 〈〈〈〈〈 represents 　　　　14.____

    A. stone   B. steel   C. glass   D. wood

15. On a heating piping drawing, the symbol ―/―/―/―/― represents piping. 　　　　15.____

    A. high-pressure steam   B. medium-pressure steam
    C. low-pressure   D. hot water supply

16. Of the following devices, the one that is LEAST frequently used to attach a piece of 　　　　16.____
equipment to concrete or masonry walls is a(n)

    A. carriage bolt   B. through bolt
    C. lag screw   D. expansion bolt

17. A vapor barrier is usually installed in conjunction with 　　　　17.____

    A. drainage piping   B. roof flashing
    C. building insulation   D. wood sheathing

Questions 18-20.

DIRECTIONS: Questions 18 through 20 are to be answered in accordance with the following table

	Man Days Borough 1 Oct. Nov.		Man Days Borough 2 Oct. Nov.		Man Days Borough 3 Oct. Nov.		Man Days Borough 4 Oct. Nov.	
Carpenter	70	100	35	180	145	205	120	85
Plumber	95	135	195	100	70	130	135	80
House Painter	90	90	120	80	85	85	95	195
Electrician	120	110	135	155	120	95	70	205
Blacksmith	125	145	60	180	205	145	80	125

18. In accordance with the above table, if the average daily pay of the five trades listed above 　　　　18.____
is $47.50, the approximate labor cost of work done by the five trades during the month of
October for Borough 1 is MOST NEARLY

    A. $22,800   B. $23,450   C. $23,750   D. $26,125

19. In accordance with the above table, the Borough which MOST NEARLY made up 22.4%   19.____
of the total plumbing work force for the month of November is Borough

    A. 1   B. 2   C. 3   D. 4

20. In accordance with the above table, the average man days per month per Borough spent   20.____
on electrical work for all Boroughs combined is MOST NEARLY

    A. 120   B. 126   C. 130   D. 136

21. Of the following percentages of carbon, the one that would indicate a medium carbon   21.____
steel is

    A. 0.2%   B. 0.4%   C. 0.8%   D. 1.2%

22. A *screw pitch gage* measures only the   22.____

    A. looseness of threads
    B. tightness of threads
    C. number of threads per inch
    D. gage number

23. Assume that you are to make an inspection of a building to determine the need for paint-   23.____
ing.
Of the following tools, the one which is LEAST needed to aid you in your inspection is a

    A. sharp penknife   B. putty knife
    C. lightweight tack hammer   D. six-foot rule

24. A *slump test* for concrete is used MAINLY to measure the concrete's   24.____

    A. strength   B. consistency   C. flexibility   D. porosity

25. Specifications which contain the term *kiln dried* would MOST likely refer to   25.____

    A. asphalt shingles   B. brick veneer
    C. paint lacquer   D. lumber

26. In accordance with established jurisdictional work procedures among the trades, the per-   26.____
son you would assign to replace a malfunctioning fire sprinkler head would be a

    A. plumber   B. laborer   C. housesmith   D. steamfitter

27. Of the following types of union shops, the one which is illegal under the Taft-Hartley Law   27.____
is the _____ shop.

    A. closed   B. open
    C. union   D. union representative

28. Of the following types of contracts, the one that in city work would MOST likely be limited   28.____
to emergency work *only* is

    A. lump-sum
    B. unit-price
    C. cost-plus
    D. partial cost-plus and lump-sum

9

29. Of the following qualifications of outside work contractors, the one which is the LEAST important requirement for determining eligible contractors is   29.____

    A. availability   B. size of work force
    C. experience   D. location of business

30. Of the following piping materials, the one that combines the physical strength of mild steel with the corrosion resistance of gray iron is   30.____

    A. grade A steel   B. grey cast iron
    C. welded wrought iron   D. ductile iron

31. Assume that a can of red lead paint needs to be thinned slightly. Of the following, the one that should be used is   31.____

    A. turpentine   B. lacquer thinner
    C. water   D. alcohol

32. Assume that a trench is 42" wide, 5' deep, and 100' long. If the unit price of excavating the trench is $35 per cubic yard, the cost of excavating the trench is MOST NEARLY   32.____

    A. $2,275   B. $5,110   C. $7,000   D. $21,000

33. Of the following uses, the one for which a bituminous compound would usually be used is to   33.____

    A. prevent corrosion of burled steel tanks
    B. increase the strength of concrete
    C. caulk water pipes
    D. paint inside wood columns

34. An electrical drawing is drawn to a scale of 1/4" = 1'. If a length of conduit on the drawing measures 7 3/8", the actual length of the conduit, in feet, is MOST NEARLY   34.____

    A. 7.5'   B. 15.5'   C. 22.5'   D. 29.5'

35. Of the following steam heating systems, the one that operates under both vacuum and low pressure conditions, without using a vacuum pump, is generally known as a _____ system.   35.____

    A. one pipe low pressure   B. vacuum
    C. vapor   D. high pressure

36. Of the following valve trim symbols, the one which designates a valve trim made of monel material is   36.____

    A. 8-18   B. NI-CU   C. SM   D. MI

37. A replacement part for a piece of equipment is to be made of S.A.E. 4047 steel. This material is MOST likely a _____ steel.   37.____

    A. wrought   B. nickel
    C. chrome-vanadium   D. molybdenum

38. A metallic underground water piping system is to be used as a means of grounding.   38.____
    Of the following statements concerning use of this system, the one that is MOST
    NEARLY CORRECT is that this use is

    A. not permitted
    B. permitted where available
    C. absolutely required
    D. permitted only in certain cases

39. For pipe sizes up to 8", schedule 40 pipe is identical to _____ pipe.   39.____

    A. standard   B. extra strong
    C. double extra strong   D. type M copper

40. Assume that a shop is undergoing a general housecleaning, and all excess unused   40.____
    materials have been removed. *Clean-up work,* as pertains to painting in this case, means
    MOST NEARLY

    A. a thorough two-coat paint job
    B. only that surface which was marred to be painted
    C. a one-coat job to *freshen things up*
    D. only that iron work is to be painted

41. The *United States Standard Gage* is used to measure sheet metal thicknesses of   41.____

    A. iron and steel   B. aluminum
    C. copper   D. tin

42. Headers and stretchers are used in the construction of   42.____

    A. floors   B. walls   C. ceilings   D. roofs

Questions 43-44.

DIRECTIONS: Questions 43 and 44, inclusive, are to be answered in accordance with the fol-
               lowing paragraph.

   *For cast iron pipe lines, the middle ring or sleeve shall have <u>beveled</u> ends and shall be
high quality cast iron. The middle ring shall have a minimum wall thickness of 3/8" for pipe up
to 8", 7/16" for pipe 10" to 30", and 1/2" for pipe over 30", nominal diameter. Minimum length
of middle ring shall be 5" for pipe up to 10", 6" for pipe 10" to 30", and 10" for pipe 30" nominal
diameter and larger. The middle ring shall not have a center pipe stop, unless otherwise
specified.*

43. As used in the above paragraph, the word *beveled* means MOST NEARLY   43.____

    A. straight   B. slanted   C. curved   D. rounded

44. In accordance with the above paragraph, the middle ring of a 24" nominal diameter pipe   44.____
    would have a minimum wall thickness and length of _____ thick and _____ long.

    A. 3/8"; 5"   B. 3/8"; 6"   C. 7/16"; 6"   D. 1/2"; 6"

11

45. A work order is NOT usually issued for which one of the following jobs: 45._____

    A. Repairing wood door frames
    B. Taking daily inventory
    C. Installing electric switches in maintenance shop
    D. Repairing a number of valves in boiler room

46. Of the following statements, the one which usually does NOT pertain to preventative 46._____
maintenance programs is

    A. periodic inspection of facilities
    B. lubrication of equipment
    C. minor repair of equipment
    D. complete replacement of deteriorated equipment

Questions 47-50.

DIRECTIONS: Questions 47 through 50, inclusive, are based on the sketch of metal sheet
shown below. (Sketch not to scale.)

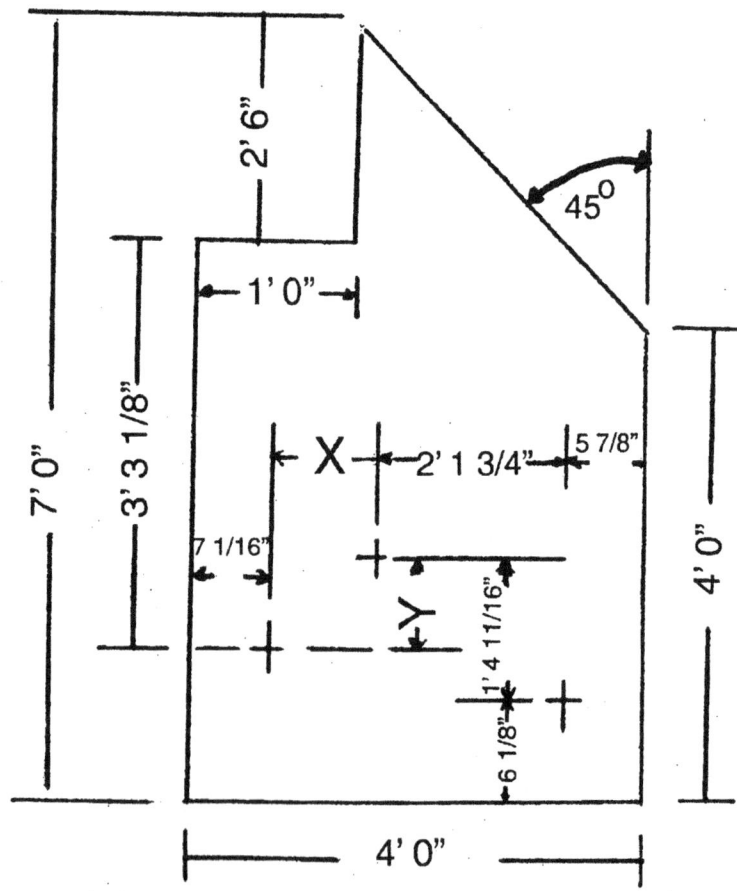

47. From the above sketch, the distance marked **X** is MOST NEARLY 47._____

    A. 5 1/4"   B. 6 5/16"   C. 7 1/8"   D. 9 5/16"

48. From the above sketch, the distance marked **Y** is MOST NEARLY

    A. 5 11/16"   B. 6 3/16"   C. 7 5/16"   D. 8 11/16"

48.____

49. In reference to the above sketch, if each piece is made from a rectangular piece of metal measuring 4' x 7', the percent of waste material is MOST NEARLY

    A. 10%   B. 15%   C. 25%   D. 30%

49.____

50. In reference to the above sketch, if the metal is 1/4" thick and weighs 144 pounds per cubic foot, the net weight of one piece would be MOST NEARLY _____ pounds.

    A. 51   B. 63   C. 75   D. 749

50.____

KEY (CORRECT ANSWERS)

1. C	11. A	21. B	31. A	41. A
2. D	12. C	22. C	32. A	42. B
3. A	13. A	23. D	33. A	43. B
4. D	14. D	24. B	34. D	44. C
5. C	15. B	25. D	35. C	45. B
6. B	16. A	26. D	36. B	46. D
7. C	17. C	27. A	37. D	47. D
8. C	18. C	28. C	38. B	48. D
9. D	19. B	29. D	39. A	49. C
10. A	20. B	30. D	40. C	50. B

EXAMINATION SECTION
TEST 1

DIRECTIONS: Each question or incomplete statement is followed by several suggested answers or completions. Select the one that BEST answers the question or completes the statement. *PRINT THE LETTER OF THE CORRECT ANSWER IN THE SPACE AT THE RIGHT.*

1. A maintenance man complains to you that he is getting all the boring jobs to do. You   1.____
    check and find that his complaint has no basis in fact.
    The one of the following which is the MOST likely reason why the maintenance man
    made such a claim is that he

    A.   wants to get even with the supervisor
    B.   lives in a world of fantasy
    C.   believes the injustice to be real
    D.   is jealous of other workers

2. When on preliminary review of a mechanic's written grievance you feel the grievance to   2.____
    be unfounded, the FIRST step you should take is to

    A.   show the mechanic where he is wrong
    B.   check carefully to find out why the mechanic thinks that way
    C.   try to humor the mechanic out of it
    D.   tell the mechanic to stop complaining

3. Assume that you decide to hold a private meeting with one of your mechanics who has a   3.____
    drinking problem that is affecting his work.
    At the meeting, the BEST way for you to handle this situation is to

    A.   tell the mechanic off and then listen to what he has to say
    B.   criticize the mechanic's behavior to get him to *open up* in order to help him correct
         his problem quickly
    C.   try to get the mechanic to recognize his problem and find ways to solve it
    D.   limit the discussion to matters concerning only the problem and look for immediate
         results

4. The one of the following which is a generally accepted guide in criticizing a subordinate   4.____
    EFFECTIVELY is to

    A.   criticize the improper act, not the individual
    B.   put the listener on the defensive
    C.   make the criticism general instead of specific
    D.   correct the personality, not the situation

5. The one of the following disciplinary methods by which you are MOST likely to be suc-   5.____
    cessful in getting a problem employee to improve his behavior is when you

    A.   discipline the employee in front of others
    B.   consider the matter to be ended after the disciplining
    C.   give the exact same discipline no matter how serious the wrongdoing
    D.   make an example of the employee

15

6. Of the following statements, the one that is MOST applicable to a disciplinary situation is   6.____
   that discipline should be

   A. used after a cooling-off period
   B. identical for all employees
   C. consistent with the violation
   D. based on personal feelings

7. The one of the following approaches that is MOST important for you to take in evaluating   7.____
   a mechanic in order to increase his work productivity is to

   A. first have him evaluate his own performance
   B. meet with him to discuss how he is doing and what is expected on the job
   C. send him a copy of your evaluation of his work performance and give him the
      opportunity to submit written comments
   D. express in writing your appreciation of his work

8. Assume that you say to one of the mechanics, *Jim, that job you turned out today was*   8.____
   top-notch. I didn't think you could do so well with the kind of material you had to work
   with.
   This statement BEST describes an example of your

   A. recognition of the man's work
   B. disrespect for the man's feelings
   C. personal favoritism of the man
   D. constructive criticism of the man's work

9. In general, the OUTSTANDING characteristic of employees over 50 years of age is their   9.____

   A. resistance   B. endurance
   C. wisdom   D. job stability

10. You should be interested in the morale of your men because morale is MOST often asso-   10.____
    ciated with

    A. mechanization   B. automation
    C. production   D. seniority regulations

11. Assume that the maintenance work order system is about to be changed. Your workers   11.____
    would MOST likely show the LEAST resistance to this change if you

    A. downgrade the old maintenance work order system
    B. tell your workers how the change will benefit them
    C. post the notice of the change on the bulletin board
    D. tell the workers how the change will benefit management

12. Of the following, the BEST way to motivate a newly appointed mechanic is to   12.____

    A. explain the meaning of each assignment
    B. make the work more physically demanding
    C. test the mechanic's ability
    D. use as much authority as possible

13. The one of the following which is the LEAST important reason for giving employees information concerning policy changes which will affect them is that employees should know   13._____

    A. why the change is being made
    B. who will be affected by the change
    C. when the change will go into effect
    D. how much savings will be made by the change

14. A foreman who knows how to handle his men will MOST likely get them to produce more by treating them   14._____

    A. alike   B. as individuals
    C. on a casual basis   D. as a group

15. Of the following items, the one that a supervisor has the MOST right to expect from his employees is   15._____

    A. liking the job
    B. a fair day's work
    C. equal skill of all mechanics
    D. perfection

16. The one of the following which is the BEST practice for you to follow in handling a dispute between the workers is to   16._____

    A. side with one of the workers so as to end the dispute quickly
    B. pay no attention to the dispute and let the workers settle it themselves
    C. listen to each worker's story of the dispute and then decide how to settle it
    D. discuss the dispute with other workers and then decide how to settle it

17. You are likely to run into an employee morale problem when assigning a dirty job that comes up often.
Of the following, the BEST method of assigning this work is to   17._____

    A. rotate this assignment
    B. assign it to the fastest worker
    C. assign it by seniority
    D. assign it to the least skilled worker

18. Of the following, the one that is generally regarded as the BEST aid to high work productivity of subordinates is a supervisor's skill in   18._____

    A. record keeping
    B. technical work
    C. setting up rules and regulations
    D. human relations

19. The BEST way to help a mechanic who comes to you for advice on a personal problem is to   19._____

    A. listen to the worker's problem without passing judgment
    B. tell the worker to forget about the problem and to stop letting it interfere with his work
    C. talk about your own personal problems to the worker
    D. mind your own business and leave the worker alone

20. You are in charge of the maintenance shop and have learned that within the next two weeks the maintenance shop will be moved to a new location on the plant grounds, but you have not learned why this move is taking place. Assume that you have decided not to keep this information from your mechanics until the reason is known but to inform them of this matter now.
Of the following, which one is the BEST argument that can be made regarding your decision?

    A. *Acceptable;* because although the reason is not now known, the mechanics will eventually find out about the move
    B. *Unacceptable;* because the mechanics do not know at this time the reason for the move and this will cause anxiety on their part
    C. *Acceptable*; because the mechanics will be affected by the move and they should be told what is happening
    D. *Unacceptable;* because the mechanics' advance knowledge of the move will tend to slow down their work output

20.____

21. Of the following, the FIRST action for a foreman to take in making a decision is to

    A. get all the facts
    B. develop alternate solutions
    C. get opinions of others
    D. know the results in advance

21.____

22. Assume that you have just been promoted to foreman.
Of the following, the BEST practice to follow regarding your previous experience at the mechanic's level is to

    A. continue to fraternize with your old friends
    B. use this experience to better understand those who now work for you
    C. use your old connections to keep top management informed of mechanics' views
    D. forget the mechanics' points of view

22.____

23. You have decided to hold regular group discussions with your subordinates on various aspects of their duties.
Of the following methods you might use to begin such a program, the one which is likely to be MOST productive is to

    A. express your own ideas and persuade the group to accept them
    B. save time and cover more ground by asking questions calling for yes or no answers
    C. propose to the group a general plan of action rather than specific ideas carefully worked out
    D. provide an informal atmosphere for the exchange of ideas

23.____

24. The principle of learning by which a foreman might get the BEST results in training his subordinates is:

    A. Letting the learner discover and correct his own mistakes
    B. Teaching the most technical part of the work first
    C. Teaching all parts of the work during the first training session
    D. Getting the learner to use as many of his five senses as possible

24.____

25. A new mechanic is to be trained to do an involved operation containing several steps of varying difficulty. This mechanic will MOST likely learn the operation more quickly if he is taught   25._____

   A. each step in its proper order
   B. the hardest steps first
   C. the easiest steps first
   D. first the steps that do not require tools

KEY (CORRECT ANSWERS)

1.	C		11.	B
2.	B		12.	A
3.	C		13.	D
4.	A		14.	B
5.	B		15.	B
6.	C		16.	C
7.	B		17.	A
8.	A		18.	D
9.	D		19.	A
10.	C		20.	C

21.	A
22.	B
23.	D
24.	D
25.	C

TEST 2

DIRECTIONS: Each question or incomplete statement is followed by several suggested answers or completions. Select the one that BEST answers the question or completes the statement. *PRINT THE LETTER OF THE CORRECT ANSWER IN THE SPACE AT THE RIGHT.*

1. The one of the following job situations in which it is better to give a written order than an oral order is when

    A. the job involves many details
    B. you can check the job's progress easily
    C. the job is repetitive in nature
    D. there is an emergency

1.____

2. Which one of the following serves as the BEST guideline for you to follow for effective written reports?
Keep sentences

    A. short and limit sentences to one thought
    B. short and use as many thoughts as possible
    C. long and limit sentences to one thought
    D. long and use as many thoughts as possible

2.____

3. Of the following, the BEST reason why a foreman generally should not do the work of an individual mechanic is that

    A. the shop's production figures will not be accurate
    B. a foreman is paid to supervise
    C. the foreman must maintain his authority
    D. the employee may become self-conscious

3.____

4. One method by which a foreman might prepare written reports to management is to begin with the conclusions, results, or summary and to follow this with the supporting data.
The BEST reason why management may prefer this form of report is because

    A. management lacks the specific training to understand the data
    B. the data completely supports the conclusions
    C. time is saved by getting to the conclusions of the report first
    D. the data contains all the information that is required for making the conclusions

4.____

5. Forms used for time records and work orders are important to the work of a foreman PRIMARILY because they give him

    A. the knowledge of and familiarity with work operations
    B. the means of control of personnel, material, or job costs
    C. the means for communicating with other workers
    D. a useful method for making filing procedures easier

5.____

6. The one of the following which is the MOST important factor in determining the number   6._____
of employees you can effectively supervise is the

    A. type of work to be performed
    B. priority of the work to be performed
    C. salary level of the workers
    D. ratio of permanent employees to temporary employees

7. Of the following, you will be MOST productive in carrying out your supervisory responsi-   7._____
bilities if you

    A. are capable of doing the same work as your mechanics
    B. meet with your mechanics frequently
    C. are very friendly with your mechanics
    D. get work done through your mechanics

8. You have been asked to prepare the annual budget for your maintenance shop.   8._____
The one of the following which is the FIRST step you should take in preparing this budget is to determine the

    A. amount of maintenance work which is scheduled for the shop
    B. time it takes for a specific unit of work to be completed
    C. current workload of each employee in the shop
    D. policies and procedures of the shop's operations

9. When determining the amount of work you expect a group of mechanics to perform in a   9._____
given time, the BEST procedure for you to follow should be to

    A. aim for a higher level of production than that of the most productive worker
    B. stay at the present production level
    C. set general instead of specific goals
    D. let workers participate in the determination whenever possible

10. You have been asked to set next year's performance goals concerning the ratio of jobs   10._____
completed on schedule to total jobs worked. A review of last year's record shows that the
workers completed their jobs on schedule 85% of the time, with the best ones showing
an on-time ratio of 92% and the poorest ones showing an on-time ratio of 65%.
Using these facts in line with generally accepted goal-setting practices, you should set
a performance ratio for the next year on the basis of _____ average with a _____
minimum acceptable for any employee.

    A. 85%; 65%   B. 85%; 70%   C. 90%; 65%   D. 90%; 70%

11. It is important for you to be able to identify the critical parts of a large project such as the   11._____
remodeling of your maintenance shop.
The one of the following which is the BEST reason why this is important is that it may

    A. help you to set up good communications between you and your workers
    B. give you a better understanding of the purpose of the project
    C. give you control over the time and cost involved in the project
    D. help you to determine who are your most productive workers

12. When doing work planning for your shop, the factor that you should normally consider LAST among the following is knowing your   12.____

    A. major objectives   B. record keeping system
    C. minor objectives   D. priorities

13. You have the responsibility for ordering all materials for your maintenance shop. A listing   13.____
of materials needed for the operations of your shop is long overdue. You realize that you are unable to find time to take care of the inventory personally because of a high priority project you have been working on which has been taking all of your time. You do not know when you will be finished with the project.
The BEST of the following courses of action to take in handling this inventory matter is to

    A. request that you be taken off the project immediately so that you may take care of the inventory
    B. complete your high priority project and then do the inventory yourself
    C. volunteer to work overtime so that you may complete the inventory while continuing with the project
    D. assign the inventory work to a competent subordinate

14. You have the authority and responsibility for seeing that proper records are kept in your   14.____
shop. Assume that you decide to delegate to a records clerk the responsibility for collecting the time sheets and the authority to make changes on the time sheets to correct the information when necessary.
Of the following, which one is the BEST argument that can be made regarding your decision?

    A. *Unacceptable*; because you can delegate only your responsibility but none of your authority to the records clerk
    B. *Acceptable*; because you can delegate some of your authority and some of your responsibility to the records clerk
    C. *Unacceptable*; because you can delegate only your authority but none of your responsibility to the records clerk
    D. *Acceptable*; because you can delegate all your responsibility and all your authority to the records clerk

15. You will LEAST likely be able to do an effective job of controlling operating costs if you   15.____

    A. eliminate idle time   B. reduce absenteeism
    C. raise your budget   D. combine work operations

16. Of the following actions, the one which is LEAST likely to help in carrying out your   16.____
responsibilities of looking after the interests of your workers is to

    A. crack down on your workers when necessary
    B. let your workers know that you support company policy
    C. prevent the transfers of your workers
    D. back up your workers in a controversy

17. The term *accountability*, as used in management of supervision, means MOST NEARLY   17.___

    A. responsibility for results   B. record keeping
    C. bookkeeping systems   D. inventory control

18. Assume that you have been unable to convince an employee of the seriousness of his poor attendance record by talking to him.
The one of the following which is the BEST course of action for you to take is to

    A. keep talking to the employee
    B. recommend that a written warning be given
    C. consider transferring the employee to another work location
    D. recommend that the employee be fired

18._____

19. When delegating work to a subordinate foreman, you should NOT

    A. delegate the right to make any decisions
    B. be interested in the results of the work, but in the method of doing the work
    C. delegate any work that you can do better than your subordinate
    D. give up your final responsibility for the work

19._____

20. Of the following statements, the BEST reason why proper scheduling of maintenance work is important is that it

    A. eliminates the need for individual job work orders
    B. classifies job skills in accordance with performance
    C. minimizes lost time in performing any maintenance job
    D. determines needed repairs in various locations

20._____

21. Of the following factors, the one which is of LEAST importance in determining the number of subordinates that an individual should be assigned to supervise is the

    A. nature of the work being supervised
    B. qualifications of the individual as a supervisor
    C. capabilities of the subordinates
    D. lines of promotion for the subordinates

21._____

22. Suppose that a large number of semi-literate residents of this city have been requesting the assistance of your department. You are asked to prepare a form which these applicants will be required to fill out before their requests will be considered.
In view of these facts, the one of the following factors to which you should give the GREATEST amount of consideration in preparing this form is the

    A. size of the form
    B. sequence of the information asked for on the form
    C. level of difficulty of the language used in the form
    D. number of times which the form will have to be reviewed

22._____

23. A budget is a plan whereby a goal is set for future operations. It affords a medium for comparing actual expenditures with planned expenditures.
The one of the following which is the MOST accurate statement on the basis of this statement is that

    A. the budget serves as an accurate measure of past as well as future expenditures
    B. the budget presents an estimate of expenditures to be made in the future
    C. budget estimates should be based upon past budget requirements
    D. planned expenditures usually fall short of actual expenditures

23._____

24. A foreman who is familiar with modern management principles should know that the one   24.____
of the following requirements of an administrator which is LEAST important is his ability
to

    A. coordinate work
    B. plan, organize, and direct the work under his control
    C. cooperate with others
    D. perform the duties of the employees under his jurisdiction

25. The one of the following which should be considered the LEAST important objective of   25.____
the service rating system is to

    A. rate the employees on the basis of their potential abilities
    B. establish a basis for assigning employees to special types of work
    C. provide a means of recognizing superior work performance
    D. reveal the need for training as well as the effectiveness of a training program

---

KEY (CORRECT ANSWERS)

1.	A	11.	C
2.	A	12.	B
3.	B	13.	D
4.	C	14.	B
5.	B	15.	C
6.	A	16.	C
7.	D	17.	A
8.	A	18.	B
9.	D	19.	D
10.	D	20.	C

21.	D
22.	C
23.	B
24.	D
25.	A

EXAMINATION SECTION
TEST 1

DIRECTIONS: Each question or incomplete statement is followed by several suggested answers or completions. Select the one that BEST answers the question or completes the statement. *PRINT THE LETTER OF THE CORRECT ANSWER IN THE SPACE AT THE RIGHT.*

1. The combustion efficiency of a boiler can be determined with a CO_2 indicator and the   1.____

    A. under fire draft   B. boiler room humidity
    C. flue gas temperature   D. outside air temperature

2. A quick, practical method of determining if the cast-iron waste pipe delivered to a job has been damaged in transit is to   2.____

    A. hydraulically test it
    B. "ring" each length with a hammer
    C. drop each length to see whether it breaks
    D. visually examine the pipe for cracks

3. An electrostatic precipitator is used to   3.____

    A. filter the air supply
    B. remove sludge from the fuel oil
    C. remove particles from the fuel gas
    D. supply samples for an Orsat analysis

4. The PRIMARY cause of cracking and spalling of refractory lining in the furnace of a steam generator is *most likely* due to   4.____

    A. continuous over-firing of boiler
    B. slag accumulation on furnace walls
    C. change in fuel from solid to liquid
    D. uneven heating and cooling within the refractory brick

5. The term "effective temperature" in air conditioning means   5.____

    A. the dry bulb temperature
    B. the average of the wet and dry bulb temperatures
    C. the square root of the product of wet and dry bulb temperatures
    D. an arbitrary index combining the effects of temperature, humidity, and movement

6. The piping in all buildings having dual water distribution systems should be identified by a color coding of _____ for potable water lines and _____ for non-potable water lines.   6.____

    A. green; red   B. green; yellow
    C. yellow; green   D. yellow; red

7. The breaking of a component of a machine subjected to excessive vibration is called   7.____

    A. tensile failure   B. fatigue failure
    C. caustic embrittlement   D. amplitude failure

8. The TWO MOST important factors to be considered in selecting fans for ventilating systems are   8.____

    A. noise and efficiency
    B. space available and weight
    C. first cost and dimensional bulk
    D. construction and arrangement of drive

9. In the modern power plant deaerator, air is removed from water to   9.____

    A. reduce heat losses in the heaters
    B. reduce corrosion of boiler steel due to the air
    C. reduce the load of the main condenser air pumps
    D. prevent pumps from becoming vapor bound

10. The abbreviations BOD, COD, and DO are associated with   10.____

    A. flue gas analysis   B. air pollution control
    C. boiler water treatment   D. water pollution control

11. The piping of a newly installed drainage system should be tested upon completion of the rough plumbing with a head of water of NOT LESS THAN _____ feet.   11.____

    A. 10   B. 15   C. 20   D. 25

12. Of the following statements concerning aquastats, the one which is CORRECT is: 12.____

    A. Aquastats may be obtained with either a narrow or wide range of settings
    B. Aquastats have a mercury tube switch which is controlled by the stack switch
    C. An aquastat is a device used to shut down the burner in the event of low water in the boiler
    D. An aquastat should be located about 4 inches above the normal water line of the boiler

13. The SAFEST way to protect the domestic water supply from contamination by sewage or non-potable water is to insert   13.____

    A. air gaps
    B. swing connections
    C. double check valves
    D. tanks with overhead discharge

14. The MAIN function of a back-pressure valve which is sometimes found in the connection between a water drain pipe and the sewer system is to   14.____

    A. equalize the pressure between the drain pipe and the sewer
    B. prevent sewer water from flowing into the drain pipe
    C. provide pressure to enable waste to reach the sewer
    D. make sure that there is not too much water pressure in the sewer line

15. Boiler water is neutral if its pH value is   15.____

    A. 0   B. 1   C. 7   D. 14

16. A domestic hot water mixing or tempering valve should be preceded in the hot water line   16.____
    by a

    A. strainer   B. foot valve
    C. check valve   D. steam trap

17. Between a steam boiler and its safety valve there should be   17.____

    A. no valve of any type
    B. a gate valve of the same size as the safety valve
    C. a swing check valve of at least the same size as the safety valve
    D. a cock having a clear opening equal in area to the pipe connecting the boiler and
         safety valve

18. A diagram of horizontal plumbing drainage lines should have cleanouts shown   18.____

    A. at least every 25 feet
    B. at least every 100 feet
    C. wherever a basin is located
    D. wherever a change in direction occurs

19. When a Bourdon gauge is used to measure steam pressures, some form of siphon or   19.____
    water seal must be maintained.
    The reason for this is to

    A. obtain "absolute" pressure readings
    B. prevent steam from entering the gage
    C. prevent condensate from entering the gage
    D. obtain readings below atmospheric pressure

20. In a closed heat exchanger, oil is cooled by condensate which is to be returned to a   20.____
    boiler. In order to avoid the possibility of contaminating the condensate with oil should a
    tube fail in the oil cooler, it would be good practice to

    A. cool the oil by air instead of water
    B. treat the condensate with an oil solvent
    C. keep the oil pressure in the exchanger higher than the water pressure
    D. keep the water pressure in the exchanger higher than the oil pressure

21. A radiator thermostatic trap is used on a vacuum return type of heating system to   21.____

    A. release the pocketed air only
    B. reduce the amount of condensate
    C. maintain a predetermined radiator water level
    D. prevent the return of live steam to the return line

22. According to the color coding of piping, fire protection piping should be painted   22.____

    A. green   B. yellow   C. purple   D. red

23. The MAIN purpose of a standpipe system is to   23.____

    A. supply the roof water tank
    B. provide water for firefighting

C. circulate water for the heating system
D. provide adequate pressure for the water supply

24. The name "Saybolt" is associated with the measurement of   24._____

A. viscosity   B. Btu content
C. octane rating   D. temperature

25. Recirculation of conditioned air in an air-conditioned building is done MAINLY to   25._____

A. reduce refrigeration tonnage required
B. increase room entrophy
C. increase air specific humidity
D. reduce room temperature below the dewpoint

26. In a plumbing installation, vent pipes are GENERALLY used to   26._____

A. prevent the loss of water seal from traps by evaporation
B. prevent the loss of water seal due to several causes other than evaporation
C. act as an additional path for liquids to flow through during normal use of a plumb-ing fixture
D. prevent the backflow of water in a cross-connection between a drinking water line and a sewage line

27. The designation "150 W" cast on the bonnet of a gate valve is an indication of the   27._____

A. water working temperature
B. water working pressure
C. area of the opening in square inches
D. weight of the valve in pounds

28. In the city, the size soil pipe necessary in a sewage drainage system is determined by the   28._____

A. legal occupancy of the building
B. vertical height of the soil line
C. number of restrooms connected to the soil line
D. number of "fixture units" connected to the soil line

29. Fins or other extended surfaces are used on heat exchanger tubes when   29._____

A. the exchanger is a water-to-water exchanger
B. water is on one side of the tube and condensing steam on the other side
C. the surface coefficient of heat transfer on both sides of the tube is high
D. the surface coefficient of heat transfer on one side of the tube is low compared to the coefficient on the other side of the tube

30. A fusible plug may be put in a fire tube boiler as an emergency device to indicate low water level. The fusible plug is installed so that under normal operating conditions,   30._____

A. both sides are exposed to steam
B. one side is exposed to water and the other side to steam
C. one side is exposed to steam and the other side to hot gases
D. one side is exposed to the water and the other side to hot gases

31. Extra strong wrought-iron pipe, as compared to standard wrought-iron pipe of the same nominal size, has

    A. the same outside diameter but a smaller inside diameter
    B. the same inside diameter but a larger outside diameter
    C. a larger outside diameter and a smaller inside diameter
    D. larger inside and outside diameters

31._____

32. Fans may be rated on a dynamic or a static efficiency basis. The dynamic efficiency would *probably* be

    A. lower in value because of the energy absorbed by the air velocity
    B. the same as the static in the case of centrifugal blowers running at various speeds
    C. the same as the static in the case of axial flow blowers running at various speeds
    D. higher in value than the static

32._____

33. The function of the stack relay in an oil burner installation is to

    A. regulate the draft over the fire
    B. regulate the flow of fuel oil to the burner
    C. stop the motor if the oil has not ignited
    D. stop the motor if the water or steam pressure is too high

33._____

34. The type of centrifugal pump which is inherently balanced for hydraulic thrust is the

    A. double suction impeller type
    B. single suction impeller type
    C. single stage type
    D. multistage type

34._____

35. The specifications for a job using sheet lead calls for "4-lb. sheet lead."
    This means that each sheet should weigh

    A. 4 lbs.   B. 4 lbs. per square
    C. 4 lbs. per square foot   D. 4 lbs. per cubic inch

35._____

36. The total cooling load design conditions for a building are divided for convenience into two components.
    These are:

    A. infiltration and radiation
    B. sensible heat and latent heat
    C. wet and dry bulb temperatures
    D. solar heat gain and moisture transfer

36._____

37. The function of a Hartford loop used on some steam boilers is to

    A. limit boiler steam pressure
    B. limit temperature of the steam
    C. prevent high water levels in the boiler
    D. prevent back flow of water from the boiler into the return main

37._____

38. Vibration from a ventilating blower can be prevented from being transmitted to the duct work by

    A. installing straighteners in the duct
    B. throttling the air supply to the blower
    C. bolting the blower tightly to the duct
    D. installing a canvas sleeve at the blower outlet

38.____

39. A specification states that access panels to suspended ceiling will be of metal. The MAIN reason for providing access panels is to

    A. improve the insulation of the ceiling
    B. improve the appearance of the ceiling
    C. make it easier to construct the building
    D. make it easier to maintain the building

39.____

40. A plumber on a job reports that the steamfitter has installed a 3" steam line in a location at which the plans show the house trap. On inspecting the job, you should

    A. tell the steamfitter to remove the steam line
    B. study the condition to see if the house trap can be relocated
    C. tell the plumber and steamfitter to work it out between themselves and then report to you
    D. tell the plumber to find another location for the trap because the steamfitter has already completed his work

40.____

41. In the installation of any heating system, the MOST important consideration is that

    A. all elements be made of a good grade of cast iron
    B. all radiators and connectors be mounted horizontally
    C. the smallest velocity of flow of heating medium be used
    D. there be proper clearance between hot surfaces and surrounding combustible material

41.____

42. Which one of the following is the PRIMARY object in drawing up a set of specifications for materials to be purchased?

    A. Control of quality
    B. Outline of intended use
    C. Establishment of standard sizes
    D. Location and method of inspection.

42.____

43. The drawing which should be used as a LEGAL reference when checking completed construction work is the _____ drawing.

    A. contract   B. assembly
    C. working or shop   D. preliminary

43.____

Questions 44-50.

DIRECTIONS: Questions 44 through 50 refer to the plumbing drawing shown below.

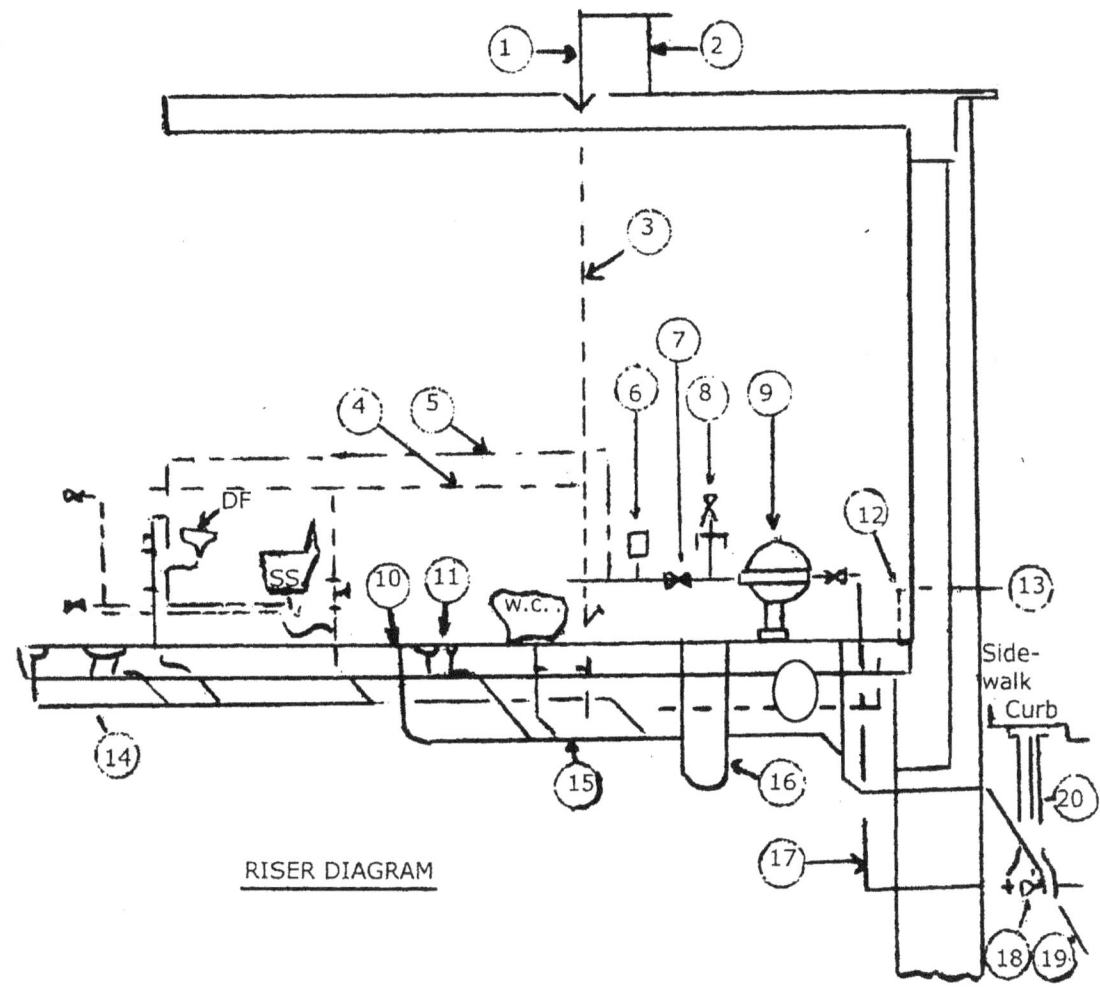

RISER DIAGRAM

44.   According to the building code, the MINIMUM diameter of No. (1) and its minimum   44._____

height, No. (2) respectively, are

    A.   2" and 12"   B.   3" and 18"
    C.   4" and 24"   D.   6" and 36"

45.   No (6) is a   45._____

    A.   relief valve   B.   shock absorber
    C.   testing connection   D.   drain

46.   No. (9) is a   46._____

    A.   strainer   B.   float valve
    C.   meter   D.   pedestal

47.   No. (11) is a   47._____

    A.   floor drain   B.   cleanout
    C.   trap   D.   vent connection

48. No. ⑬ is a

    A. standpipe
    C. sprinkler head

    B. air inlet
    D. cleanout

48.____

49. The size of No. ⑯ is

    A. 2" x 2"
    C. 3" x 3"

    B. 2" x 3"
    D. 4" x 4"

49.____

50. No. ⑱ is a

    A. pressure reducing valve
    B. butterfly valve
    C. curb cock
    D. sprinkler head

50.____

————————

KEY (CORRECT ANSWERS)

1.	C	11.	A	21.	D	31.	A	41.	D
2.	B	12.	C	22.	D	32.	D	42.	A
3.	C	13.	A	23.	B	33.	C	43.	A
4.	D	14.	B	24.	A	34.	A	44.	C
5.	D	15.	C	25.	A	35.	C	45.	B
6.	B	16.	A	26.	B	36.	B	46.	C
7.	B	17.	A	27.	B	37.	D	47.	A
8.	A	18.	D	28.	D	38.	D	48.	B
9.	B	19.	B	29.	D	39.	D	49.	D
10.	D	20.	D	30.	D	40.	B	50.	C

————————

EXAMINATION SECTION
TEST 1

DIRECTIONS: Each question or incomplete statement is followed by several suggested answers or completions. Select the one that BEST answers the question or completes the Statement. *PRINT THE LETTER OF THE CORRECT ANSWER IN THE SPACE AT THE RIGHT.*

1.   What type of pump has a diffusion *ring?*

   A.   Centrifugal   B.   Duplex double acting
   C.   Helical gear   D.   Spur gear

1._____

2.   A cause of excessive oil consumption in an air compressor is

   A.   oil with improper viscosity
   B.   defective discharge valve
   C.   oil level too high in oil sump
   D.   loose unloader unit

2._____

3.   How does cylinder oil compare with engine oil at engine room temperature? Cylinder oil

   A.   is lighter in color
   B.   has a higher viscosity
   C.   has a lower viscosity
   D.   is lighter when put in front of a light

3._____

4.   On a boiler-feed centrifugal pump, to maintain a certain speed, 60 horsepower is used. To double that speed, so as to obtain double the output, how much horsepower is needed?

   A.   120   B.   240   C.   360   D.   480

4._____

5.   The *slip* of a pump refers to

   A.   lost motion on the steam slide valve
   B.   leakage past the plunger on an outside packed pump
   C.   recirculation of liquid from discharge side back to suction side
   D.   clearance when piston is slipped inside cylinder

5._____

6.   On a reciprocating vacuum pump, the diameter of the steam piston is _____ the liquid piston.

   A.   larger than   B.   smaller than
   C.   the same size as   D.   twice the diameter of

6._____

7.   How many valves are there on the water end of a duplex double-acting feed pump?

   A.   8   B.   6   C.   4   D.   2

7._____

8. Which of the following would you find on a duplex pump?

    A. Springs and packing
    B. Gears and impeller
    C. Flywheel and crank
    D. Crankshaft and air chamber

8.____

9. The function of the air chamber on a duplex, double-acting pump is to

    A. prevent hammering
    B. increase capacity of pump
    C. aerate the water
    D. prevent cavitation

9.____

10. The valve discs on the water end of a duplex pump are USUALLY made of

    A. wood   B. steel
    C. rubber   D. cast iron

10.____

11. A direct-acting, duplex steam pump *short strokes* when it returns from overhaul. The PROBABLE cause is

    A. feed water too cold
    B. steam pressure too low
    C. steam valves not properly set
    D. water discharge pressure too high

11.____

12. A heavy duty pump is one which

    A. is designed for the pumping of heavy liquids
    B. pumps large quantities of water
    C. has a high thermal efficiency
    D. is made of extra heavy material for high head pressure

12.____

13. When a punch is used in making holes for rivets or boiler tubes, the diameter of the punch shall be _____ the desired hole.

    A. three-quarters of the diameter of
    B. slightly smaller than
    C. exactly the same size as
    D. slightly larger than

13.____

14. On a _____ pump, you would find a *volute*.

    A. reciprocating   B. centrifugal
    C. jet   D. direct-pressure

14.____

15. In starting a centrifugal boiler feed pump with 300 lbs. water pressure on the line, the valves should be set with suction _____ and discharge _____.

    A. open; open   B. open; closed
    C. closed; closed   D. closed; open

15.____

16. On a centrifugal boiler feed pump, the regulating valve functions to maintain

    A. speed constant   B. pressure constant
    C. variable speed   D. water level

16.____

17. With centrifugal pumps, the head varies directly as the   17.____

    A. speed   B. speed squared
    C. speed cubed   D. diameter squared

18. An intercooler is used on a   18.____

    A. compound engine   B. two-stage air compressor
    C. two-stage turbine   D. two-stage evactor

19. The unloader on an air compressor is provided for   19.____

    A. reducing pressure   B. easy starting
    C. high-starting pressure   D. reducing temperature

20. A duplex center outside a packed feed water pump has   20.____

    A. yoke rod   B. two water plungers
    C. compound steam glands   D. four water pistons

21. A centrifugal pump operates with a high suction lift, which would require _____ line.   21.____

    A. lift check at bottom of suction
    B. swing check in discharge
    C. stop valve in discharge
    D. lift check at top of suction

22. Diffuser vanes will MOST generally be found in a _____ pump.   22.____

    A. centrifugal turbine   B. centrifugal volute
    C. rotary   D. reciprocating

23. A sewer ejector would be located   23.____

    A. on the roof of a building
    B. in the basement
    C. in the sub-basement
    D. in the sewer

24. How many pots are there on a double-acting water pump?   24.____

    A. 1   B. 2   C. 3   D. 4

25. What is the amount of steam consumption of a simple, duplex steam pump, in lbs./H.P. hour?   25.____

    A. 5-20   B. 25-35   C. 50-90   D. 120-200

KEY (CORRECT ANSWERS)

1.	A		11.	C
2.	C		12.	D
3.	B		13.	D
4.	D		14.	B
5.	B		15.	A
6.	B		16.	D
7.	A		17.	B
8.	A		18.	B
9.	A		19.	A
10.	C		20.	B

21. A
22. A
23. C
24. D
25. A

TEST 2

DIRECTIONS: Each question or incomplete statement is followed by several suggested answers or completions. Select the one that BEST answers the question or completes the statement. *PRINT THE LETTER OF THE CORRECT ANSWER IN THE SPACE AT THE RIGHT.*

1. The type of valve on a duplex steam pump is   1.____

     A. sleeve   B. piston
     C. D-slide valve   D. poppet

2. The slide valve on a Knowles pump is operated by   2.____

     A. linkage attached to the piston rod
     B. rocker arm of opposite steam slide
     C. an auxiliary piston
     D. discharge water pressure

3. A duplex, double-acting pump with the valves properly adjusted will   3.____

     A. not start sometimes
     B. always start
     C. jig
     D. start when off dead center

4. If one valve stem of a duplex, double-acting pump broke, the pump would   4.____

     A. increase in speed   B. run slower
     C. stop   D. run on one side only

5. The diameter of the steam cylinders of an 18 x 16 x 24 duplex, direct-acting steam pump is _____ inches.   5.____

     A. 18   B. 16   C. 24   D. 30

6. On a boiler feed pump, the   6.____

     A. steam cylinder is always larger than the water cylinder
     B. water cylinder is always larger than the steam cylinder
     C. cylinders are of equal size
     D. water discharge pipe is always larger than the suction pipe

7. Flax packing is used for   7.____

     A. steam end of pump
     B. water end of pump
     C. between flanges of pipe lines
     D. high temperature

8. Water is dripping out of the gland of a centrifugal pump used to pump feed water. You should   8.____

     A. renew the packing at the first opportunity
     B. pull up the gland as tight as possible with an ordinary 6 inch pipe wrench

C. pull up the gland just to the point where water does not leak out
D. do nothing

9. On the initial tightening of a jam-type gland on a boiler-feed water pump to stop excessive leakage, you would pull up alternately on the hexagonal nuts _____ turn.

    A. 1/6   B. 1/2   C. 3/4   D. 1 full

9.____

10. Diffuser vanes will MOST generally be found in a _____ pump.

    A. centrifugal turbine   B. centrifugal volute
    C. rotary   D. reciprocating

10.____

11. If the consumption of lubricating oil in an air compressor is excessive, it is MOST likely due to

    A. using too high viscosity oil
    B. a defective discharge valve
    C. a loose unloader unit
    D. oil too high in sump

11.____

12. Which of the following statements is CORRECT about a Worthington steam-driven duplex double-acting boiler feed pump?

    A. Will always start in position in which it was stopped
    B. Will not start if stopped with one piston at extreme head end and other at dead center
    C. Speed is controlled by inertia type governor
    D. Dust of f must always be 25%

12.____

13. Centrifugal boiler feed pumps for large boilers with fluctuating loads are usually fitted with a system for recirculating or recycling.
This is done to prevent

    A. excessive head pressure
    B. loss of suction
    C. excessing governor action
    D. overheating with consequent flashing and seizing of the pump

13.____

14. In the operation of a turbo-driven centrifugal pump, the delivery of the pump would PROPERLY be controlled by

    A. throttling the discharge
    B. throttling the suction
    C. using a bypass
    D. throttling the steam supply

14.____

15. Assume that it is necessary to pump 40 M.G.D. against a 65 ft. head.
If the pump efficiency is 65%, the B.H.P. of this pump is MOST NEARLY

    A. 920   B. 700   C. 460   D. 176

15.____

16. Assume that a pump had to be shut down temporarily due to trouble which was first reported by an oiler.
    The one of the following entries in the log concerning this occurrence which is LEAST important is

    16.____

    A. time of the shutdown
    B. period of time the pump was out of service
    C. cause of the trouble
    D. time the oiler came on shift

17. At sea level, the theoretical maximum distance, in feet, the water can be lifted by suction *only* is MOST NEARLY

    17.____

    A. 12.00　　　　B. 14.70　　　　C. 33.57　　　　D. 72.00

18. While a lubricating oil is in use, for good performance, its neutralization number should

    18.____

    A. keep rising
    C. be greater than 0.1
    B. remain about the same
    D. be greater than 2.0

19. The parts of a large sewage pump that would MOST likely need repairs after the fewest number of hours of operation are the

    19.____

    A. pump casings
    C. wearing rings
    B. impellers
    D. outboard bearings

20. Flexible coupling used to connect a pump to an electric motor valve is USUALLY rated in horsepower per

    20.____

    A. 100 rpm of shaft
    B. 300 rpm of shaft
    C. square inch of shaft area
    D. inch of shaft diameter

KEY (CORRECT ANSWERS)

1.	C	11.	D
2.	B	12.	A
3.	B	13.	D
4.	C	14.	D
5.	A	15.	B
6.	A	16.	D
7.	B	17.	C
8.	D	18.	B
9.	A	19.	C
10.	A	20.	A

EXAMINATION SECTION
TEST 1

DIRECTIONS: Each question or incomplete statement is followed by several suggested answers or completions. Select the one that BEST answers the question or completes the statement. *PRINT THE LETTER OF THE CORRECT ANSWER IN THE SPACE AT THE RIGHT.*

1. To check for the entrance of toxic wastes into a treatment plant, each of the following may be reliably observed as indicators EXCEPT   1.____

    A. changes in color of incoming wastewater
    B. waste recording equipment
    C. odors
    D. bulking of sludge in the clarifier

2. An increase in _____ could cause a demand for more oxygen in an aeration tank.   2.____

    A. inert or inorganic wastes
    B. pH
    C. toxic substances
    D. microorganisms

3. Chlorine may be added for hydrogen sulfide control in the   3.____

    A. collection lines   B. aeration tank
    C. plant effluent   D. trickling filter

4. The range of typical carrying capacities, in gallons per minute, of intermediate pumping stations is   4.____

    A. less than 600   B. 200-700
    C. 100-1,600   D. 700-10,000

5. A low sulfanator injector vacuum reading could be caused by   5.____

    A. missing gasket
    B. high back pressure
    C. high-volume injector flow
    D. wrong orifice

6. Before starting a rotating biological contactor process, each of the following should be checked EXCEPT   6.____

    A. lubrication   B. biomass
    C. clearance   D. tightness

7. The capacity for water or wastewater to neutralize acids is expressed in terms of   7.____

    A. pH   B. oxygen demand
    C. alkalinity   D. acidity

8. Which of the following is NOT one of the available methods for determining stormwater flow for the purpose of storm sewer design?   8.____

   A.   Rainfall and runoff correlation studies
   B.   Inlet method
   C.   Hydrograph method
   D.   Outlet method

9.   What is the term for the accumulation of residue that appears on trickling filters and must be removed periodically?   9.____

   A. Sludges   B. Slurries   C. Slugs   D. Sloughings

10.   A sludge containing a high number of living organisms is referred to as   10.____

   A. raw   B. activated   C. primary   D. toxic

11.   Which of the following is NOT a plant location where liquid mixing is commonly practiced?   11.____

   A.   Ponds
   B.   Hydraulic jumps in open channels
   C.   Pipelines
   D.   Venturi flumes

12.   Which of the following industries releases primarily inorganic wastes in its effluent?   12.____

   A. Paper   B. Petroleum
   C. Gravel washing   D. Dairy

13.   Which of the following collection system variables could upset a plant's activated sludge process?   13.____

   A.   Discharge by industrial cleaning operations
   B.   Chlorination of return sludge flows
   C.   Decreases in influent flows
   D.   Recycling of digester supernatant

14.   The second-stage BOD is also referred to as the _____ stage.   14.____

   A. carbonaceous   B. pretreatment
   C. flocculation   D. nitrification

15.   When organic matter decomposes to form foul-smelling products associated with the lack of free oxygen, this condition is known as   15.____

   A. shock loading   B. septicity
   C. sloughing   D. sidestreaming

16.   Which type of bacteria has the HIGHEST optimum temperature for treatment?   16.____

   A. Mesophilic   B. Cryophilic
   C. Thermophilic   D. Psychrophilic

17.   The COD test   17.____

   A.   estimates the total oxygen consumed
   B.   measures the carbon oxygen demand
   C.   provides results more quickly than the BOD test
   D.   measures only the nitrification oxygen demand

18. Which of the following is NOT considered a major factor that may cause variations in lab test results?   18.____

    A. The nature of the material being examined
    B. Testing equipment
    C. Sampling procedures
    D. The quantity of material being examined

19. The treatment process that MOST effectively removes suspended solids from wastewater is   19.____

    A. sedimentation   B. flocculation
    C. skimming   D. comminution

20. Which of the following is a thickening alternative in sludge processing?   20.____

    A. Flotation   B. Incineration
    C. Elutriation   D. Wet oxidation

21. The device that continuously adds the flow of wastewater into a plant is the   21.____

    A. aggregate   B. turbidity meter
    C. titrator   D. totalizer

22. Two types of measurement required in connection with the operation of a treatment plant are   22.____

    A. effluent and downstream
    B. temperature and dissolved oxygen
    C. in-plant and receiving water
    D. temperature and receiving water

23. You may NOT dispose of excess activated sludge waste from package plants   23.____

    A. at a nearby treatment plant
    B. by anaerobic digestion
    C. by removal by septic tank pumper
    D. by aeration in a holding tank, then deposit in a sanitary landfill

24. What is the term for the combination of activated sludge with raw wastewater in a treatment plant?   24.____

    A. Median   B. Liquefaction
    C. Effluent   D. Mixed liquor

25. Landfills produce poisonous _____ gas as a byproduct of decomposition.   25.____

    A. methane   B. nitrogen
    C. chlorofluorocarbons   D. argon

KEY (CORRECT ANSWERS)

1.	B		11.	A
2.	D		12.	C
3.	A		13.	A
4.	D		14.	D
5.	B		15.	B
6.	B		16.	C
7.	C		17.	C
8.	D		18.	D
9.	D		19.	B
10.	B		20.	A

21.	D
22.	C
23.	B
24.	D
25.	A

TEST 2

DIRECTIONS: Each question or incomplete statement is followed by several suggested answers or completions. Select the one that BEST answers the question or completes the statement. *PRINT THE LETTER OF THE CORRECT ANSWER IN THE SPACE AT THE RIGHT.*

1. Which of the following types of pumps is a kinetic pump?   1.____

    A. Rotary   B. Piston plunger
    C. Hydraulic ram   D. Blow case

2. What device is used to keep floated solids out of the effluent in dissolved air flotation thickeners?   2.____

    A. Cloth screens   B. Microscreens
    C. Effluent baffles   D. Water sprays

3. The _____ is NOT one of the primary factors affecting the flow of wastewater and sewage in sewers.   3.____

    A. viscosity of the liquid
    B. cross-sectional area of the system conduit
    C. time of day
    D. pipe surface

4. What is the term for washing a digested sludge in the plant effluent?   4.____

    A. Masking   B. Elutriation
    C. Hydrolysis   D. Slaking

5. _____ is NOT an objective in periodically pumping sludge from the primary clarifier to the digester.   5.____

    A. Prevention of pump clogging
    B. Prevention of digester overload
    C. Allowance for thicker sludge pumping
    D. Maintenance of good clarifier conditions

6. The toxic chemical LEAST likely to be encountered by treatment plant operators is(are)   6.____

    A. mercury   B. acids
    C. fluorocarbons   D. bases

7. Which concentration of total dissolved solids, in milligrams per liter, would be the MINIMUM required in order to be considered *strong* in wastewater?   7.____

    A. 250   B. 500   C. 850   D. 1,200

8. What is the term for the treatment process in which a tank or reactor is filled, the water is treated, and the tank is emptied?   8.____

    A. Flocculation   B. Centration
    C. Batch process   D. Pond process

9. The mixing of a compound with water to produce a true chemical reaction is to   9.____

    A. dissolve   B. slake   C. strip   D. hydrate

10. If the difference in elevation between inflow and outflow sewers is greater than 1.5 feet, which device is needed?   10._____

   A. Side weir   B. Drop inlet
   C. Baffles   D. Inlet casting

11. Intermittent releases or discharges of industrial wastes are known as   11._____

   A. slurries   B. slugs   C. splashes   D. stop logs

12. Results from the settleability test of activated sludge solids may be used to   12._____

   A. calculate BOD
   B. determine probable flow rates at which sludges may clog equipment
   C. calculate sludge age
   D. determine ability of solids to separate from liquid in final clarifier

13. The device used to measure the temperature of an effluent is a   13._____

   A. thermometer   B. Bourdon tube
   C. thermocouple   D. pug mill

14. Which source is typically the HEAVIEST contributor of total solids in a service area's wastewater supply?   14._____

   A. Industrial wastes   B. Domestic wash waters
   C. Storm runoff   D. Human biological wastes

15. The term for liquid removed from a settled sludge is   15._____

   A. hydrolyte   B. supernatant
   C. aliquot   D. slurry

16. A unit of wastewater moving through the treatment system without dispersing or mixing with the rest of the wastewater in the system is called   16._____

   A. centration   B. plug flow
   C. putrefaction   D. slugging

17. What is the term for the groups or clumps of bacteria or particles that have clustered together during the treatment process?   17._____

   A. Coagulants   B. Slurries
   C. Floes   D. Slugs

18. The purpose of PRIMARY sedimentation is to remove   18._____

   A. settleable and floatable material
   B. roots, rags, and large debris
   C. suspended and dissolved solids
   D. sand and gravel

19. _____ would NOT cause an increase in effluent coliform levels at a treatment plant.   19._____

   A. Mixing problems
   B. An increase in effluent BOD
   C. Solids accumulation in the contact chamber
   D. High chlorine residual

20. What is the term used to describe bacteria that can live under either aerobic or anaerobic conditions?   20.____

   A. Cultured   B. Agglomerated
   C. Filamentous   D. Facultative

21. Which devices are NOT used during pretreatment?   21.____

   A. Racks   B. Comminutors
   C. Screens   D. Coagulators

22. Through which stage in an activated sludge treatment plant would wastewater pass FIRST?   22.____

   A. Grit chambers   B. Bar racks
   C. Settling tanks   D. Primary sedimentation

23. The inorganic gas LEAST likely to be found around a treatment plant is   23.____

   A. ammonia   B. methane
   C. hydrogen sulfide   D. mercaptans

24. The soils in an effluent disposal on land program may be tested using each of the following procedures EXCEPT   24.____

   A. BOD   B. conductivity
   C. pH   D. cation exchange capacity

25. Which of the following is a conditioning alternative in sludge processing?   25.____

   A. Centrifugation   B. Drying
   C. Composing   D. Elutriation

KEY (CORRECT ANSWERS)

1. C	11. B
2. C	12. D
3. C	13. C
4. B	14. A
5. A	15. B
6. C	16. B
7. C	17. C
8. C	18. A
9. B	19. D
10. B	20. D

21. D
22. B
23. D
24. A
25. D

EXAMINATION SECTION
TEST 1

DIRECTIONS: Each question or incomplete statement is followed by several suggested answers or completions. Select the one that BEST answers the question or completes the statement. *PRINT THE LETTER OF THE CORRECT ANSWER IN THE SPACE AT THE RIGHT.*

1. To measure the diameter of a replacement pump shaft, a(n) _____ should be used.   1.____

    A. surveyor's chain   B. micrometer
    C. metallic tape   D. engineer's scale

2. A _____ is used to bypass storm flow in a combined-sewerage system.   2.____

    A. drop inlet   B. side weir
    C. hydraulic jump   D. baffle

3. The PRIMARY element in a control system is the   3.____

    A. transmitter   B. receiver
    C. sensor   D. controller

4. The use of water to break down complex substances into simpler ones is called   4.____

    A. dissolving   B. hydrolysis
    C. coagulation   D. hydrostasis

5. In its progress through a pumping station, wastewater FIRST passes through a   5.____

    A. comminutor   B. chlorine room
    C. wet well   D. barminutor

6. Which of the following is NOT one of the main operational factors for a barminutor?   6.____

    A. Amount of debris in wastewater
    B. Number of units in service
    C. Head loss through unit
    D. Removal of floatables

7. Which of the following precautions must be taken before attempting to repair a surface aerator?   7.____

    A. Shut down aerator
    B. Drain aeration tank
    C. Secure header assembly
    D. Test atmosphere for toxic gases

8. Which of the following source types would MOST likely influence the pH of wastewater?   8.____

    A. Industrial   B. Commercial
    C. Agricultural   D. Domestic

9. Each of the following items should be carefully controlled in an activated sludge plant in order to prevent sludge bulking EXCEPT   9.____

    A. filamentous growth   B. length of aeration time
    C. return sludge rate   D. sludge age

10. Sludge blanket depths may be measured by the use of

    A. ultrasonic transmitters and receivers
    B. pressure gages
    C. floats connected to cables
    D. bubbler tubes

10.____

11. The vertical distance from the normal water surface to the top of the confining wall of a pond or tank is called the

    A. freeboard   B. force main
    C. header   D. stop log

11.____

12. Suspended solids in the effluent from a trickling filter plant may be caused by

    A. heavy sloughing from the filters
    B. precipitation of solids in the secondary filter
    C. condensation of effluent on secondary equipment
    D. flotation of solids in the primary clarifier

12.____

13. What is MOST often produced during the decomposition of domestic wastes?

    A. Phenols   B. Oxygen
    C. Hydrogen sulfide   D. Sulfur

13.____

14. Air compressor vibration sensing devices are used to measure each of the following EXCEPT

    A. flow   B. velocity
    C. acceleration   D. displacement

14.____

15. The height or energy of liquids above a certain point is measured in terms of

    A. discharge rate   B. volume
    C. flow   D. head

15.____

16. Factors in the design of sanitary sewers include each of the following EXCEPT

    A. maximum rate for an entire service area's domestic sewage within a specified time period
    B. maximum rates from commercial and industrial areas
    C. infiltration allowance for entire service area
    D. maximum rates from domestic and industrial/commercial sources combined

16.____

17. Which of the following could prevent a pump from starting?

    A. Tripped circuit breakers
    B. Air leaks in suction line
    C. High discharge head
    D. Lack of priming

17.____

18. Through which stage would wastewater undergoing chemical-physical treatment pass FIRST?

    A. Precipitation   B. Stripping
    C. Flocculation   D. Slaking

18.____

19. Which of the following could be considered a normal operating condition for micro-screens?   19.____

    A. High flow   B. High pH level
    C. Low pH flow   D. Toxic wastes

20. The tank in which sludges are placed in order to allow decomposition is known as the   20.____

    A. emulsion   B. dessicator
    C. digester   D. percolator

21. The conversion of large solid sludge particles into fine particles that can be dissolved or suspended in water is called   21.____

    A. hydrolysis   B. liquefaction
    C. comminution   D. recirculation

22. A mixture in which two or more liquid substances are held in suspension is called a(n)   22.____

    A. solution   B. electrolyte
    C. emulsion   D. reagent

23. What is the term for a mass of sludge containing a highly concentrated population of microorganisms?   23.____

    A. Septic   B. Seed
    C. Shock load   D. Slug

24. Which of the following forms of nitrogen is LEAST important to the wastewater treatment process?   24.____

    A. Nitrate   B. Ammonia   C. Elemental   D. Organic

25. What is the term for water leaving a centrifuge after the removal of most solids?   25.____

    A. Cation exchange   B. Centration
    C. Flocculation   D. Turbidity

KEY (CORRECT ANSWERS)

1.	B		11.	A
2.	B		12.	A
3.	C		13.	C
4.	B		14.	A
5.	C		15.	D
6.	D		16.	D
7.	A		17.	A
8.	A		18.	C
9.	D		19.	D
10.	A		20.	C

21.	B
22.	C
23.	B
24.	C
25.	B

TEST 2

DIRECTIONS: Each question or incomplete statement is followed by several suggested answers or completions. Select the one that BEST answers the question or completes the statement. *PRINT THE LETTER OF THE CORRECT ANSWER IN THE SPACE AT THE RIGHT.*

1. The MOST effective treatment process for destroying or removing bacteria from waste-water is through

   A.   activated sludge process
   B.   trickling filter
   C.   chlorination
   D.   sedimentation

1.____

2. Which of the following tasks is NOT associated with the starting of a comminutor?

   A.   Check positioning of inlet and outlet gases
   B.   Inspect for frayed cables
   C.   Adjust cutter blades
   D.   Inspect for lubrication and oil leaks

2.____

3. One of the objectives of digester mixing is

   A.   the use of waste gas to run mixers
   B.   adequate cooling throughout digester contents
   C.   the release of hydrogen sulfide gas
   D.   microorganic inoculation of raw sludge

3.____

4. Which type of bacteria would give the STRONGEST indication of the possible presence of pathogenic bacteria in waste-water?

   A.   Coliform   B.   Filamentous
   C.   Heterotrophic   D.   Facultative

4.____

5. Cryogenic oxygen plants should be shut down for maintenance every

   A.   six months   B.   year
   C.   two years   D.   five years

5.____

6. At the _____ stage in the biological treatment process, aerobic bacteria uses dissolved oxygen to convert carbon compounds to carbon dioxide.

   A.   clarifying   B.   carbonaceous
   C.   nitrification   D.   coagulation

6.____

7. _____ is NOT an influential factor in the settleability of solids in a clarifier.

   A.   Detention time
   B.   Flow velocity
   C.   The movement of sludge scrapers
   D.   Temperature

7.____

8. Which concentration of total organic carbon, in milligrams per liter, would be considered *moderate* in wastewater?   8._____

    A. 50   B. 100   C. 200   D. 300

9. Which of the following is a volume reduction alternative in sludge processing?   9._____

    A. Centrifugation   B. Chemical conditioning
    C. Flotation   D. Drying

10. The hydraulic loading for a phosphate stripper depends on the   10._____

    A. dissolved oxygen of the activated sludge
    B. pH of wastewater
    C. BOD loading of the unit
    D. ability of the aerobic phosphate stripper to remain aerobic

11. The range of typical carrying capacities, in gallons per minute, of package-plant pumping stations is   11._____

    A. less than 600   B. 200-700
    C. 100-1,600   D. 700-10,000

12. When a sludge becomes too light and refuses to settle properly in a clarifier, this is known as   12._____

    A. centration   B. precipitation
    C. comminution   D. bulking

13. In a wet well, level control systems include each of the following EXCEPT   13._____

    A. bubblers   B. hearts   C. floats   D. electrodes

14. Which of the following is NOT one of the primary sources of odors in a wastewater treatment plant?   14._____

    A. Unwashed grit
    B. The carbon adsorption process
    C. Sludge incinerators
    D. Waste-gas burning

15. A chemical property used in the classification of irrigation waters is   15._____

    A. pH   B. total dissolved solids
    C. BOD   D. aeration

16. Which of the following is NOT a potential use for the dissolved air flotation process?   16._____

    A. Solids recovery   B. Coagulation
    C. Wastewater treatment   D. Water recovery

17. Each of the following is a principal factor determining the use of pumping stations in sewage collection EXCEPT the   17._____

    A. elevation of the area or district to be serviced
    B. location of natural drainage areas in relation to the service area
    C. cost of a pumping station
    D. cost of trunk sewer construction

18. Through which stage would wastewater undergoing chemical-physical treatment pass LAST?

    18.____

    A. Carbon adsorption
    B. Lime recovery
    C. Flocculation
    D. Slaking

19. Which of the following practices is NOT included in the maintenance of equipment in package operation plants?

    19.____

    A. Changing oil in the speed reducer
    B. Adjusting aeration equipment
    C. Washing tank walls and channels
    D. Inspecting the air-lift pump

20. What chemical solution is capable of neutralizing acids or bases without greatly altering pH?
A(n)

    20.____

    A. blank   B. alkaline   C. buffer   D. digester

21. Which of the following types of pumps is a displacement pump?

    21.____

    A. Centrifugal
    B. Electromagnetic
    C. Peripheral
    D. Diaphragm

22. A sludge whose solid portion can be separated from the liquid is referred to as

    22.____

    A. anhydrous
    B. soluble
    C. hydrolytic
    D. dewaterable

23. Which of the following could indicate that a high organic waste load has reached the activated sludge process?
A(n)

    23.____

    A. *increase* in DO residual in the aeration tank
    B. *increase* in turbidity in the effluent from the secondary chamber
    C. *decrease* in nutrients in the effluent from the secondary chamber
    D. *decrease* in aeration

24. The term for the clogging of the filtering medium or a microscreen or a vacuum filter is

    24.____

    A. corrosion
    B. head loss
    C. coagulation
    D. blinding

25. Through which stage in an activated sludge treatment plant would wastewater pass LAST?

    25.____

    A. Grit chamber
    B. Chlorine contact chamber
    C. Settling tanks
    D. Trickling filters

KEY (CORRECT ANSWERS)

1.	C		11.	B
2.	B		12.	D
3.	D		13.	B
4.	A		14.	B
5.	B		15.	B
6.	B		16.	B
7.	C		17.	C
8.	C		18.	A
9.	D		19.	A
10.	A		20.	C

21.	D
22.	D
23.	B
24.	D
25.	B

EXAMINATION SECTION
TEST 1

DIRECTIONS: Each question or incomplete statement is followed by several suggested answers or completions. Select the one that BEST answers the question or completes the statement. *PRINT THE LETTER OF THE CORRECT ANSWER IN THE SPACE AT THE RIGHT.*

1. Assume that a certain file has a safe edge. This is an edge that has   1.____

   A. no teeth
   B. the teeth pointing backward
   C. the teeth pointing forward
   D. fine criss-cross teeth

2. The one of the following which is the proper tool for threading a round rod is a   2.____

   A. tap   B. countersink   C. counterbore   D. die

3. A rasp is a   3.____

   A. type of chisel
   B. type of file cleaner
   C. type of coarse file
   D. kind of plane

4. The one of the following which is the proper tool to use to tighten a round nut which has a series of notches cut in its outer surface is a(n) _____ wrench.   4.____

   A. box   B. spanner   C. Stillson   D. monkey

5. Small leaks resulting from poor threads on steel or wrought-iron water pipes will often stop because the leaky threads are in time filled with   5.____

   A. sediment   B. stalactite   C. rust   D. soapstone

6. A metal that can be rolled or beaten into very fine sheets is said to be   6.____

   A. anodized   B. malleable   C. tempered   D. ferrous

7. To *rod* a sewer pipe means MOST likely to   7.____

   A. clean it out by means of rods
   B. keep the pipe clear of debris by placing a grating of rods at the intake
   C. support the sewer pipe with horizontal reinforcing metal rods
   D. shore up the pipe

8. Of the following abrasives, the one which is the LEAST coarse is   8.____

   A. No. 2 emery cloth
   B. crocus cloth
   C. No. 1 sandpaper
   D. No. 1/0 sandpaper

9. In order to permit free passage of water in one direction only and prevent a reversal of flow in the pipe, it is necessary to use a _____ valve.   9.____

   A. gate   B. check   C. globe   D. needle

10. Assume that a cubic foot of water contains 7 1/2 gallons. The number of gallons of water which could be contained in a rectangular tank 3 feet long, 2 feet wide, and 2 feet deep is MOST NEARLY   10.____

   A. 12   B. 45   C. 90   D. 120

11. The weight, in pounds, of a cubic foot of fresh water is MOST NEARLY   11._____

    A. 8.5   B. 32.4   C. 62.4   D. 98.6

12. The total weight, in pounds, of ten bags of Portland cement is MOST NEARLY   12._____
_____ pounds.

    A. 108   B. 187   C. 940   D. 1,200

13. If a concrete mix is said to be 1:2:4, this would mean that the mix is made up   13._____
of 1 part by 1

    A. volume of cement to 2 parts by volume of sand to 4 parts by volume of coarse aggregate
    B. volume of cement to 2 parts by volume of coarse aggregate to 4 parts by volume of sand
    C. volume of coarse aggregate to 2 parts by volume of sand to 4 parts by volume of cement
    D. weight of cement to 2 parts by weight of coarse aggregate to 4 parts by weight of sand

14. The ratio of the weight of a substance to the weight of an equal volume of water   14._____
is called the _____ of the substance.

    A. specific volume   B. specific gravity
    C. viscosity   D. fractional weight

15. Of the following, the pipe fitting which has four openings which permits   15._____
connecting a line at right angles to another line is called a(n)

    A. side outlet street L   B. double elbow
    C. tee   D. cross

16. To tighten a nut where only a short swing of the wrench handle is possible,   16._____
it is BEST to use a _____ wrench.

    A. ratchet   B. hook spanner
    C. Stillson   D. Bristo

17. Of the following, the proper tool to use to remove the burr from the inside   17._____
of a pipe is a

    A. half round file   B. reamer
    C. mandrel   D. chisel

18. Fittings commonly used with copper pipe should be made of   18._____

    A. brass   B. cast iron
    C. malleable iron   D. pure tin

19. With respect to pipe, the abbreviation I.P.S. means   19._____

    A. Internal Pipe Size   B. Iron Pipe Size
    C. Iron Pipe Shape   D. International Pipe Size

20. A Stillson wrench is the proper wrench to use when tightening a   20.____

    A. square nut   B. hexagonal nut

    C. valve gland nut   D. pipe fitting

21. The one of the following which is the proper tool to use for cutting wood along the grain is a _____ saw.   21.____

    A. rip   B. panel   C. cross-cut   D. back

22. The one of the following which is the proper tool to use to cut internal screw threads is a   22.____

    A. broach   B. die   C. tap   D. stock

23. A center punch is the proper tool used to   23.____

    A. cut out the center of a gasket

    B. dent metal prior to drilling

    C. drive nails beneath the surface of the wood

    D. punch a small hole in sheet metal

24. The one of the following knots which can be safely used for tying together the ends of two dry ropes of the same size is a   24.____

    A. granny knot   B. clove hitch

    C. half hitch   D. square knot

25. The PRIMARY purpose of a trap under a plumbing fixture is to   25.____

    A. act as a seal against sewer gas

    B. permit cleaning out the drain line

    C. permit the recovery of valuables accidentally dropped into the fixture

    D. permit the making of tests on the drain line

26. The one of the following which contains exactly 10 board feet is a board 10 feet long, inches wide, _____ inch(es) thick.   26.____

    A. 24; 1   B. 12; 2   C. 12; 1   D. 10; 1

27. Short pieces of pipe threaded on both ends are called   27.____

    A. nipples   B. couplings   C. bushing   D. sleeves

28. The unit of electrical capacitance is the   28.____

    A. ampere   B. farad   C. henry   D. cycle

29. As used in the electrical industry, BX means   29.____

    A. best grade of electrical wire

    B. type B extension wire

    C. metal greenfield

    D. insulated wires in flexible metal tubing

Questions 30-33.

DIRECTIONS: Questions 30 to 33, inclusive, are to be answered in accordance with the following paragraph.

One of the categories of nuisance is a chemical one and relates to the dissolved oxygen of the watercourse. The presence in sewage and industrial wastes of materials capable of undergoing biochemical oxidation and resulting in reduction of oxygen in the watercourse leads to a partial or complete depletion of this oxygen. This, in turn, leads to the subsequent production of malodorous products of decomposition, to the destruction of aquatic plant life and major fish life and to conditions offensive to sight and smell.

30   The word *malodorous* as used in the above paragraph means MOST NEARLY   30._____

   A. fragrant   B. fetid   C. wholesome   D. redolent

31   From the above paragraph, because of pollution, the amount of dissolved   31._____
oxygen in the waterways is

   A. released   B. multiplied   C. lessened   D. saturated

32.   The word *categories* as used in the above paragraph means MOST NEARLY   32._____

   A. divisions   B. clubs   C. symbols   D. products

33.   The word *offensive* as used in the above paragraph means MOST NEARLY   33._____

   A. pliable   B. complaint
   C. deferential   D. disagreeable

34.   The terminal voltage of 5 dry cells connected in a series is _____ of   34._____
one(each) cell.

   A. 1/5 the voltage   B. the same as the voltage
   C. 5 times the voltage   D. determined by the current

35.   If a 15 ampere fuse blows out and blows out again after inserting a new fuse,   35._____
it is BEST to

   A. replace it with a 10 ampere fustat
   B. replace it with two 10 ampere fuses connected in series
   C. replace it with a 20 ampere fuse
   D. have the circuit checked to find the trouble

36.   Ordinary soft solder is a mixture of lead and   36._____

   A. sulphur   B. brass   C. zinc   D. tin

37.   The electrolyte used in the ordinary flashlight-type dry cell is   37._____

   A. calcium chloride   B. ammonium chloride
   C. manganese dioxide   D. sulfuric acid

38. An electrical transformer is an electrical device used primarily to   38._____

    A. raise or lower A.C. voltages
    B. change the frequency of alternating current
    C. rectify currents from A.C. to D.C.
    D. change currents from D.C. to A.C.

39. Of the following, the MAIN reason for the grounding of electrical equipment and   39._____
circuits is to

    A. save power
    B. increase the voltage
    C. protect personnel from electric shock
    D. prevent serious short circuits

40. In order to properly ground portable electric hand tools, it is USUALLY necessary   40._____
to use a

    A. solenoid   B. circuit breaker
    C. fuse   D. three prong plug

41. The current in a simple electrical circuit can be calculated by dividing the   41._____
voltage by the resistance in ohms. Assume that the resistance of a certain
circuit is 60 ohms and its voltage is 120 volts, 60 cycle A.C.
The current in this circuit will be MOST NEARLY _____ ampere(s).

    A. 1/2   B. 2   C. 1   D. 30

42. The one of the following which is the MOST common type of motor that may   42._____
be used with an A.C. or D.C. source of supply is the _____ motor.

    A. shunt   B. squirrel cage
    C. compound   D. series

43. The electrolyte in the ordinary storage battery is   43._____

    A. nitric acid   B. sulphuric acid
    C. manganese dioxide   D. ammonium chloride

44. The one of the following terms which is used in expressing the rating of a   44._____
storage battery is

    A. ampere-hours   B. amperes
    C. volt-ampere   D. watt-hours

45. The size of the SMALLEST graduation on the ordinary 6-foot folding rule is   45._____
usually

    A. 1/8"   B. 1/16"   C. 1/32"   D. 1/64"

46. A given saw has 8 points per inch. This saw is PROBABLY a _____ saw.   46._____

  A. cross-cut   B. hack   C. veneer   D. back

47. Assume that it takes 6 men 8 days to do a certain job. Working at the same same speed, the number of days that it will take 4 men to do this job is

47._____

    A. 9   B. 10   C. 12   D. 14

48. The sum of 3 5/8 + 4 1/4 + 6 1/2 + 7 1/8 is

48._____

    A. 20 7/8   B. 21 1/4   C. 21 1/2   D. 22 1/8

49. The fraction which is equal to .0625 is

49._____

    A. 1/64   B. 3/64   C. 1/16   D. 5/8

50. The volume, in cubic feet, of a rectangular coal bin 8 ft. long by 5 ft. wide by 7 ft. high is MOST NEARLY

50._____

    A. 40   B. 56   C. 186   D. 280

KEY (CORRECT ANSWERS)

1. A	11. C	21. A	31. C	41. B
2. D	12. C	22. C	32. A	42. D
3. C	13. A	23. B	33. D	43. B
4. B	14. B	24. D	34. C	44. A
5. C	15. D	25. A	35. D	45. B
6. B	16. A	26. C	36. D	46. A
7. A	17. B	27. A	37. B	47. C
8. B	18. A	28. B	38. A	48. C
9. B	19. B	29. D	39. C	49. C
10. C	20. D	30. B	40. D	50. D

TEST 2

DIRECTIONS: Each question or incomplete statement is followed by several suggested answers or completions. Select the one that BEST answers the question or completes the statement. *PRINT THE LETTER OF THE CORRECT ANSWER IN THE SPACE AT THE RIGHT.*

Questions 1-7

DIRECTIONS: Questions 1 to 7, inclusive, are to be answered in accordance with the following information.

At sea level, the atmosphere can exert a pressure of 14.7 pounds per square inch. This pressure is capable of sustaining a column of water having a height equal to 14.7 pounds, multiplied by 2.304 (the height of water in feet which will exert one pound per square inch pressure). No pump built can produce a perfect vacuum. The atmospheric pressure exerting its force on the surface of the water from which suction is being taken forces the water up through the suction to the pump. From this, it is evident that the maximum height which a water pump of this type can lift water is determined ultimately by the atmospheric pressure. The tightness of the pump and its ability to create a vacuum also have a bearing.

1. The meaning of the word *vacuum* as used in the above article is a   1._____

    A. space entirely devoid of matter
    B. sealed tube filled with gas
    C. bottle-shaped vessel with a double wall
    D. cleaning device

2. With reference to the above article, if a pump could produce a perfect vacuum,   2._____
    the MAXIMUM height, in feet, that it could lift water at sea level is MOST
    NEARLY

    A. 33.9   B. 29.4   C. 23.3   D. 14.7

3. With reference to the above article, a column of water having a height of   3._____
    4.6 feet at sea level will exert a pressure of MOST NEARLY _____ pound(s)
    per square inch.

    A. 3   B. 2   C. 1   D. 1/2

4. The word *atmosphere* as used in the above article means   4._____

    A. the pull of gravity
    B. perfect vacuum
    C. the whole mass of air surrounding the earth
    D. the weight of water at sea level

5. The word *bearing* as used in the above article means MOST NEARLY   5._____

    A. direction   B. connection
    C. divergence   D. convergence

6. The word *evident* as used in the above article means MOST NEARLY   6.____

    A. disconcerting   B. obscure   C. equivocal   D. manifest

7. The word *maximum* as used in the above article means MOST NEARLY   7.____

    A. best   B. median   C. adjacent   D. greatest

8. Assume that a car travels at a constant speed of 36 miles per hour. The   8.____
speed of this car, in feet per second, is MOST NEARLY (one mile equals 5,280 ft.)

    A. 3   B. 24.6   C. 52.8   D. 879.8

9. If one-third of a 19-foot length of lumber is cut off, the length of the remaining   9.____
piece will measure APPROXIMATELY

    A. 8'8"   B. 9'8"   C. 12'8"   D. 13'8"

10. The circumference of a circle having a diameter of 10" is MOST NEARLY   10.____
_____ inches.

    A. 3.14   B. 18.72   C. 24.96   D. 31.4

11. Assume that in the purchase of paint, the seller quotes a discount of 10%.   11.____
If the price per gallon is $6.35, the actual payment in dollars per gallon is
MOST NEARLY

    A. $5.72   B. $5.95   C. $6.25   D. $6.50

12. On a 1" bolt that has 10 threads per inch, if the nut is turned 6 complete turns,   12.____
the distance, in inches, that the nut will move along the bolt is MOST NEARLY

    A. .3   B. .6   C. .9   D. 1

13. Assume that at one end of a 6-inch horizontal line, an 8-inch vertical line is   13.____
drawn at right angles to the horizontal line. The length, in inches, between the
ends of the two lines is MOST NEARLY

    A. 6   B. 8   C. 10   D. 12

Questions 14-21.

DIRECTIONS: Questions 14 to 21, inclusive, are to be answered in accordance with the following information.

In his 2012 annual report to the Mayor, the Public Works Commissioner stated that the city's basic water pollution control program begun in 1996 and costing $425 million so far would be completed in five or six years at a cost of $275 million more. However, he said, the city must spend an additional $175 million more on its marginal pollution control program to protect present and proposed beaches. Under the basic program, the city will have eliminated the last major discharges of raw sewage into the harbor. Over 800 million gallons, two thirds of the city's spent water each day, is now treated at 12 plants, to which six new plants will be added, enabling the city to treat the estimated 1.8 billion gallons that will be discharged daily in 2030. The department had about $200 million worth of municipal construction under way in 2012, and completed $85.5 millions' worth.

14. According to the above, the city will add _____ new plants.

    A. 18   B. 12   C. 6   D. 4

14.____

15. The amount of municipal construction under way in 2012 was _____ million.

    A. $85.5   B. $175   C. $200   D. $425

15.____

16. It is estimated that in 2030, the city will treat daily _____ gallons.

    A. 700 million   B. 800 million
    C. 900 million   D. 1.8 billion

16.____

17. According to the above article, the total cost of the water pollution program begun in 1996 will be _____ million.

    A. $275   B. $425   C. $700   D. $815

17.____

18. According to the above article, to protect present and proposed beaches, the city must spend an additional _____ million.

    A. $175   B. $275   C. $425   D. $450

18.____

19. The above article concerns the statements of the Commissioner of Public Works in his _____ annual report to the Mayor.

    A. 1996   B. 2002   C. 2012   D. 2013

19.____

20. The word *discharged* as used in the above article means MOST NEARLY

    A. emitted   B. erased   C. refuted   D. repelled

20.____

21. The word *pollution* as used in the above article means MOST NEARLY

    A. condensation   B. purification
    C. contamination   D. distillation

21.____

22. A tool commonly used to cut off the head of a rivet is a

    A. cold chisel   B. cape chisel   C. band saw   D. file

22.____

23. A metal washer is MOST often used with a _____ screw.

    A. wood   B. lag   C. hand   D. machine

23.____

24. A good safety rule to follow is that water should NOT be used to extinguish fires in or around electrical apparatus. Of the following, the PRIMARY reason for this is that water

    A. will damage the insulation
    B. will corrode the electrical conductors
    C. may cause the circuit fuse to blow
    D. may conduct electric current and cause a shock hazard

24.____

25. One should be extremely careful to keep open flames and sparks away from storage batteries when they are being charged because the

    A. sulphate given off during this operation is highly flammable
    B. hydrogen given off during this operation is highly flammable
    C. oxygen given off during this operation is extremely flammable
    D. static electricity of the battery may cause combustion

25.____

26. A good safety rule to follow is that an electric hand tool, such as a portable electric drill, should never be lifted or carried by its service cord.
Of the following, the PRIMARY reason for this rule is that the

    A. tool might swing and be damaged by striking some hard object
    B. cord might be pulled off its terminals and become short circuited
    C. tool may slip out of the hand as it is hard to get a good grip on a slick rubber cord
    D. rubber covering of the cord might overstretch

26.____

27. When a man is working on a 15-foot ladder with its top placed against a wall, the MAXIMUM safe distance that he may reach out to one side of the ladder is

    A. as far out as he can reach lifting one foot off the rung for balance
    B. as far out as he can reach without bending his body more than 45 from the vertical
    C. one-third the length of the ladder
    D. as far out as his arm's length

27.____

28. When NOT in use, oily waste rags should be stored in

    A. water-tight oak barrels   B. open metal containers
    C. sealed cardboard boxes   D. self-closing, metal containers

28.____

29. Assume that one of your co-workers has suffered an electric shock. Artificial respiration should be started on him immediately if he is

    A. unconscious and breathing   B. conscious and in a daze
    C. unconscious and not breathing   D. conscious and badly burned

29.____

30. Assume that the top of a 12-foot portable straight ladder is placed against a wall but is not held by a man or fastened in any way. In order to be safe, the ladder should be placed so that the distance from the wall to the foot of the ladder is

    A. not over 3 feet   B. not over 4 feet
    C. at least 4 feet   D. at least 5 feet

30.____

31. Of the following, the one which is an acceptable method of caring for wooden ladders is to

    A. coat the ladder with clear shellac
    B. paint the ladder with red lead followed by a second coat of the desired color
    C. paint the ladder with a coat of paint of the desired color
    D. apply a sealer coat before painting with a second coat of the desired color

31.____

32. The MOST important safety precaution to follow when using an electric drill press is to

    A. wear safety shoes   B. drill at a slow speed
    C. use plenty of cutting oil   D. clamp the work firmly

32.____

33. The proper method of lifting heavy objects is to stand

    A. far enough away from the load so that, with knees bent, the back is at an angle of 45, then lift by straightening the back
    B. close to the load, with feet solidly placed and slightly apart and knees bent; then lift by straightening the legs, keeping the back as nearly vertical as possible
    C. close to the load, with feet solidly placed and far apart, knees bent; then lift by straightening the legs, keeping the body at an angle of 30°
    D. far away from the load, with knees bent and the back at an angle of 45°, then lift by straightening the knees and slowly straightening the back

33.____

34. An oilstone is often made of

    A. silicon   B. carborundum   C. tungsten   D. emery

34.____

35. To draw a circle, you should use a(n)

    A. compass   B. caliper   C. awl   D. gage

35.____

36. A *mushroomed* head is a common defect of a

    A. rivet   B. hammer
    C. chisel   D. screwdriver

36.____

37. The tool USUALLY used to drive a lag screw is a(n)

    A. open end wrench   B. Stillson wrench
    C. screwdriver   D. Allen wrench

37.____

38. It is BEST to lubricate machinery

    A. whenever you feel the oil is running low
    B. only if the machinery needs it
    C. when the machine begins to vibrate
    D. on a regular schedule

38.____

39. When repairing machinery that is to be reassembled, punch marks are often placed on parts that are next to each other.
The reason for this is to

    A. make sure you assemble the pieces in proper order
    B. make it easier to line up the parts in proper position
    C. keep count of the number of pieces that belong to this machine
    D. provide a stop so that parts cannot be assembled too tightly

39.____

Questions 40-46.

DIRECTIONS: Questions 40 to 46, inclusive, are to be answered in accordance with the following paragraph.

*At 2:30 P.M. on Monday, October 25, Mr. Paul Jones, a newly appointed Sewage
Treatment Worker, started on a routine inspectional tour of the settling tanks and other sewage
treatment works installations of the plant to which he was assigned. At 2:33 P.M., Mr. Jones
discovered a co-worker, Mr. James P. Brown, lying unconscious on the ground. Mr. Jones
quickly reported the facts to his immediate superior, Mr. Jack Rota, who immediately
telephoned for an ambulance. Mr. Rota then rushed to the site and placed a heavy woolen
blanket over the victim. Mr. Brown was taken to the Ave. H hospital by an ambulance driven by
Mr. Dave Smith, which arrived at the sewage disposal plant at 3:02 P.M. Patrolman Robert
Daly, badge number 12520, had arrived before the ambulance and recorded all the details of
the incident, including the statements of Mr. Jones, Mr. Rota, and Mr. Nick Nespola, a Stationary Engineer (Electric), who stated that he saw the victim when he fell to the ground.*

40.   The time which elapsed between the start of the sewage treatment worker's   40._____
routine inspection and the arrival of the ambulance was MOST NEARLY
_____ minutes.

A. 3   B. 28   C. 29   D. 32

41.   The name of the sewage treatment worker's immediate superior was   41._____

A. James P. Brown   B. Jack Rota
C. Paul Jones   D. Robert Daly

42.   The name of the patrolman was   42._____

A. James P. Brown   B. Jack Rota
C. Paul Jones   D. Robert Daly

43.   Referring to the above, the incident occurred on   43._____

A. Monday, Oct. 25   B. Monday, October 26
C. Tuesday, Oct. 25   D. Tuesday, October 26

44.   The victim was found at exactly   44._____

A. 2:30 A.M.   B. 2:33 P.M.   C. 2:33 A.M.   D. 2:30 P.M.

45.   The sewage treatment worker's name was   45._____

A. James P. Brown   B. Jack Rota
C. Paul Jones   D. Dave Smith

46.   The man named Nick Nespola was the   46._____

A. Stationary Engineer (Electric)   B. patrolman
C. victim   D. ambulance driver

47. When sharpening a tool on a grindstone, the tool is often dipped in water. The MAIN reason for this is to

47.____

    A. prevent overheating of the tool   B. lubricate the grindstone
    C. produce a sharper edge on the tool   D. anneal the tool

48. It is BEST to use a screwdriver having a square shank

48.____

    A. when clearance is limited
    B. on sheet metal screws
    C. on small screws
    D. where a wrench is to be used to help turn the screwdriver

49. Brass liners are often placed over the jaws of a bench vise to

49.____

    A. grip the work better
    B. prevent damage to the work
    C. protect the vise
    D. make it easier to adjust the work

50. Other than the bulb, the part of a fluorescent light that must be changed MOST often as it wears is the

50.____

    A. switch   B. ballast   C. control   D. starter

KEY (CORRECT ANSWERS)

1. A	11. A	21. C	31. A	41. B
2. A	12. B	22. A	32. D	42. D
3. B	13. C	23. D	33. B	43. A
4. C	14. C	24. D	34. B	44. B
5. B	15. C	25. B	35. A	45. C
6. D	16. D	26. B	36. C	46. A
7. D	17. C	27. D	37. A	47. A
8. C	18. A	28. D	38. D	48. D
9. C	19. C	29. C	39. B	49. B
10. D	20. A	30. A	40. D	50. D

EXAMINATION SECTION
TEST 1

DIRECTIONS: Each question or incomplete statement is followed by several suggested answers or completions. Select the one that BEST answers the question or completes the statement. *PRINT THE LETTER OF THE CORRECT ANSWER IN THE SPACE AT THE RIGHT.*

1. The flow of sewage into the treatment plant is USUALLY controlled by a   1.____

    A. gate valve   B. sluice gate
    C. tainter gate   D. parshall gate

2. Regulator gates USUALLY close when the sewage in the interceptor sewer reaches a   2.____
    predetermined

    A. velocity   B. pressure
    C. temperature   D. elevation

3. A bar screen serves the same purpose as a   3.____

    A. filter   B. grit collector
    C. trash rack   D. sluice gate

4. Material that is removed from the sewage by the fine screen is MOST frequently   4.____

    A. blown by compressed air to the grit storage tank
    B. ground up and returned to the sewage
    C. burnt as fuel for the plant
    D. dried in the sludge drying beds and then disposed at sea

5. The one of the following pieces of equipment that is operated in conjunction with air pres-   5.____
    sure is a(n)

    A. centrifugal pump   B. venturi
    C. ejector   D. sump pump

6. One of the methods used to prime a centrifugal pump is to   6.____

    A. raise the air pressure in the pump
    B. bleed the suction line
    C. apply a vacuum to the pump
    D. open the suction valve

7. The one of the following types of pumps MOST frequently used to pump thickened   7.____
    sludge is the _____ type.

    A. ejector   B. centrifugal
    C. gear   D. piston

8. A plant is called an *Activated Sludge Plant* when the   8.____

    A. thickened sludge can be used as fertilizer
    B. gases from the sludge digestion tanks are burnt as fuel
    C. sludge must be dried before being disposed
    D. partly treated sewage is mixed with sludge

9. Where a digester tank has either a floating or a rising cover, it is made airtight by means   9._____
   of a(n)

    A. water seal   B. sliding rubber gasket
    C. leather *bellows*   D. oiled steel ring

10. Grease and fats are USUALLY removed from the sewage by   10._____

    A. skimming the liquid in the sedimentation tanks
    B. pumping the liquid from the sump in the grit chamber
    C. decanting the liquid in the digestion tank
    D. backwashing the fine screens

11. The type of plant in which *flocculation* MOST frequently occurs is the _____ plant.   11._____

    A. aerated sludge   B. chemical precipitation
    C. plain screening   D. filtration

12. Chlorine leaks are BEST detected by use of   12._____

    A. orthotoludin   B. litmus paper
    C. ammonia   D. copperas

13. Settling tanks operate effectively by _____ the sewage.   13._____

    A. slowing the speed of
    B. increasing the speed of
    C. changing the direction of flow of
    D. adding air to

14. A *venturi* is used in a sewage treatment plant in order to   14._____

    A. clean the diffusers
    B. control the amount of sewage in the wet well
    C. measure the flow of sewage
    D. reduce the pressure of the gases used as fuel

15. Sludge tanks are USUALLY heated by means of   15._____

    A. forced warm air   B. hot water
    C. radiant heat   D. electric coils

16. Chlorine is USUALLY added to sewage by   16._____

    A. adding the gas directly to the sewage
    B. mixing a small quantity of the sewage with the chlorine and then adding the mix-
        ture to the main body of sewage
    C. mixing the chlorine with water, and then adding the mixture to the sewage
    D. combining the gas with the air used in the aeration tank

17. The MAIN reason for defective operation of an aeration tank is that   17._____

    A. sewage flow is too slow
    B. of clogged diffuser plates
    C. tank temperature is too low
    D. too much air is supplied

18. The type of pump that seldom requires a relief valve is MOST likely a _____ pump.   18.____

   A. reciprocating   B. gear
   C. piston   D. centrifugal

19. The MAIN purpose of a foot valve in a centrifugal pump is to   19.____

   A. prevent the liquid from flowing back down the suction line
   B. equalize the pressure on both sides of the pump
   C. make it easier to prime the pump
   D. block passage of material that is too large to pump

20. The MAIN reason for lubricating machinery is to   20.____

   A. lower operating temperature
   B. keep down noise and vibration
   C. reduce friction
   D. lower cost of operation

21. The one of the following items that has the LOWEST viscosity is   21.____

   A. cup grease   B. kerosene
   C. #10 oil   D. #40 oil

22. The one of the following statements that is MOST NEARLY correct is: 22.____

   A. High speed machinery is most frequently lubricated by grease
   B. For most applications, either grease or oil can be used
   C. When in doubt, it is best to use the heavier of two grades of oil available
   D. Oil becomes *thinner* as the operating temperature increases

23. The function of a circuit breaker is MOST similar to that of a   23.____

   A. switch   B. fuse   C. rheostat   D. transformer

24. Noisy operation of a motor is MOST frequently caused by   24.____

   A. a shorted armature   B. over-voltage
   C. worn bearings   D. a grounded casing

25. Consumption of electrical energy is registered on a(n)   25.____

   A. volt-ohm meter   B. ammeter
   C. watt-hour meter   D. ohm meter

26. A dirty commutator is BEST cleaned by using   26.____

   A. sandpaper   B. soap and water
   C. emery cloth   D. kerosene

27. The one of the following items that is MOST frequently used to prevent an electric motor   27.____
   from being overloaded is a

   A. warning signal   B. governor
   C. thermal cut-out   D. rheostat

28. The one of the following metals that is MOST commonly used for outboard bearings is   28.____

   A. zinc   B. brass   C. magnesium   D. babbit

29. The use of pipe joint compound when making up a screwed joint results in a watertight   29.____
    joint and also

    A. cleans the threads   B. makes the joint hard
    C. lubricates the threads   D. prevents cross threading

30. A pipe is generally threaded by using a   30.____

    A. die   B. tap   C. yoke   D. swedge

31. The type of motor that MOST frequently does NOT use brushes is the   31.____

    A. universal type   B. series wound D.C. motor
    C. synchronous motor   D. induction motor

32. Compressed air can be used to clean generator and motor windings provided the air is   32.____

    A. heated
    B. blown at a high velocity
    C. used at a pressure of at least 90 lbs./sq.in.
    D. dry

33. The use of a cold chisel with a *mushroomed* head is   33.____

    A. *good*, because the mushrooming cushions the blow
    B. *bad*, because the head cannot be hit squarely
    C. *good*, because there is more area on the head to hit
    D. *bad*, because chips might fly from the head

34. After brass or black iron pipe has been cut, it should be   34.____

    A. counterbored   B. reamed
    C. countersunk   D. squared

35. The one of the following that is used to change the speed of certain types of electric   35.____
    motors is a (n)

    A. commutator   B. brush
    C. rheostat   D. armature

36. The type of pipe that is MOST frequently made with bell and spigot ends is   36.____

    A. brass   B. steel
    C. cast iron   D. transite

37. The one of the following that is used to connect two pipes together in a straight line is a   37.____

    A. manifold   B. divider   C. band   D. union

38. The difference between a stud and a bolt is that the stud has   38.____

    A. a finer thread   B. no head
    C. a round head   D. a coarser thread

39. A set screw is often used to   39.____

    A. bolt two pieces of flanged pipe together
    B. screw together matching parts in a motor casing
    C. clamp a piece to a work table
    D. secure a pulley to a shaft

40. Soft jaw inserts sometimes used to protect the surface of a piece of metal that is held in   40.____
a vise are MOST frequently made of

    A. zinc   B. tin   C. brass   D. pewter

41. The BEST type of wrench to use on a large square nut is a _____ wrench.   41.____

    A. monkey   B. spanner   C. stillson   D. spintite

42. The BEST method of cleaning files is to use a   42.____

    A. file card   B. knife
    C. scriber   D. fibre brush

43. The BEST lubricant to use when cutting threads on steel pipe is _____ oil.   43.____

    A. pike   B. penetrating
    C. lard   D. coal

44. The BEST type of valve to use to control the flow of liquid to a delicate gauge is a _____   44.____
valve.

    A. gate   B. needle   C. globe   D. check

45. Water hammer is caused MAINLY by   45.____

    A. pumping sewage to too high a head
    B. interrupting the flow of sewage too rapidly
    C. debris floating in the sewage
    D. excessive corrosion in the pipes

46. Suppose a centrifugal pump is pumping less sewage than it is capable of handling.   46.____
Of the following, the one that is NOT a possible reason for this is that the

    A. speed of pump is too slow
    B. pump is not properly primed
    C. stuffing box packing is defective
    D. suction line is partly clogged

47. The one of the following types of pumps that will give a smooth continuous flow of liquid   47.____
rather than a pulsating flow is the _____ type.

    A. reciprocating   B. rotary
    C. gear   D. centrifugal

48. For pumping against a very high head, the BEST type of pump to use is a _____ type.   48.____

    A. reciprocating   B. propeller
    C. mixed flow   D. centrifugal

49. To increase the volume of delivery of a reciprocating pump, USUALLY the 49.____

    A. angle of the impeller is increased
    B. inlet valve is opened wider
    C. piston stroke is lengthened
    D. discharge valve is opened wider

50. The capacity of a pump is MOST frequently expressed in 50.____

    A. cubic feet per day   B. gallons per day
    C. cubic feet per minute   D. gallons per minute

——————

KEY (CORRECT ANSWERS)

1. B	11. B	21. B	31. D	41. A
2. D	12. C	22. D	32. D	42. A
3. C	13. A	23. B	33. D	43. C
4. B	14. C	24. C	34. B	44. B
5. C	15. B	25. C	35. C	45. B
6. C	16. C	26. A	36. C	46. B
7. D	17. B	27. C	37. D	47. D
8. D	18. D	28. D	38. B	48. A
9. A	19. A	29. C	39. D	49. C
10. A	20. C	30. A	40. C	50. D

——————

TEST 2

DIRECTIONS: Each question or incomplete statement is followed by several suggested answers or completions. Select the one that BEST answers the question or completes the statement. *PRINT THE LETTER OF THE CORRECT ANSWER IN THE SPACE AT THE RIGHT.*

1. The sum of the following dimensions: 1 5/8, 2 1/4, 4 1/16, 3 3/16, is   1.____

    A.   10 15/16   B.   11   C.   11 1/8   D.   11 1/4

2. Assume that six men, working together at the same rate of speed, can complete a certain job in 3 hours.   2.____
If, however, there were only four men available to do this job, and they all worked at the same rate of speed, to complete this job would take MOST NEARLY _____ hours.

    A.   4 1/4   B.   4 1/2   C.   4 3/4   D.   5

3. Due to unforeseen difficulties, a job which would normally take 17 hours to complete was actually completed in 21 hours.   3.____
This represents a percent increase over the normal time of MOST NEARLY

    A.   19%   B.   2.4%   C.   24%   D.   124%

4. The veteran should approach the problem of safety with the idea that   4.____

    A.   there will always be accidents
    B.   most accidents can be prevented
    C.   the best method of preventing accidents is to post safety rules for the men to follow
    D.   punishing the man with the worst accident record will reduce the number of accidents occurring

5. The one of the following that is NOT a common cause of accidents occurring when working around machinery is   5.____

    A.   wearing loose clothing
    B.   wearing gloves
    C.   having insufficient illumination
    D.   having slippery floors

Questions 6-8.

DIRECTIONS: Questions 6 through 8, inclusive, are to be answered in accordance with the following information.
    A certain job requires 4 men working the number of hours and at the salary rate indicated in the accompanying table.

Name	No. of Hours	Salary/Hr.
Brown	30	$15.00
Jones	22	$19.50
Walter	40	$10.50
Thomas	25	$17.22

6. According to the above table, the salary received by Thomas on this job is MOST   6.____
   NEARLY

   A. $426.00   B. $427.50   C. $429.00   D. $430.50

7. According to the above table, the man who received the MOST wages chargeable to this   7.____
   job is

   A. Brown   B. Jones   C. Walter   D. Thomas

8. According to the above table, the total amount of wages chargeable to this job is MOST   8.____
   NEARLY

   A. $1,726.50   B. $1,717.50   C. $1,729.50   D. $1,737.50

9. Of the following statements, the one that represents the SAFEST practice in a shop is: 9.____
   Adjustments should be made on.

   A. running machinery only if another man can be assigned to guard the man making
      the actual adjustment
   B. running machinery only if proper protective equipment is worn
   C. running machinery only when the machine is grounded
   D. machinery only after the machine has been stopped

10. Regarding work performed on electrical circuits, the one of the following that is unsafe is   10.____
    to

    A. use #10 wire instead of #12
    B. ground the junction boxes
    C. replace a 15 ampere circuit breaker with a 20 ampere one
    D. open the main switch before working on the wiring

11. Of the following, the MOST important reason for making detailed reports of all accidents   11.____
    is to

    A. have a record of who to blame for the accident
    B. be able to properly assess the cost of the accident
    C. reduce the number of *compensation* claims
    D. determine the causes of accidents and eliminate future accidents

12. As a veteran sewage treatment worker, you can BEST promote safety in your operations   12.____
    by

    A. carefully investigating and reporting the circumstances of any accident
    B. suggesting safer methods of operation
    C. training subordinates in proper safety
    D. disciplining subordinates who engage in unsafe acts

13. Oil-soaked rags are BEST stored in a   13.____

    A. neat pile in a readily accessible corner
    B. metal container with a tight cover
    C. metal box that has holes for adequate ventilation
    D. closet on a shelf above the ground

14. The one of the following actions that is NOT the cause of injury when working with hand tools is   14._____

    A. working with defective tools
    B. using the wrong tool for the job
    C. working too carefully
    D. using a tool improperly

15. Artificial respiration is the FIRST action you should take when a man becomes unconscious either as a result of drowning or as a result of   15._____

    A. chlorine poisoning   B. electric shock
    C. falling   D. clothing catching fire

Questions 16-17.

DIRECTIONS: Questions 16 and 17 should be answered in accordance with the following paragraph.

Sewage treatment plants are designed so that the sewage flow reaches the plant by gravity. In some instances, a small percentage of the sewerage system may be below the planned level of the plant. Economy in construction and other factors may indicate that the raising of that lower portion of the flow by means of pumps, to the desired plant elevation, is more desirable than lowering the plant structure. Some plants operate with this feature.

16. According to the above paragraph,   16._____

    A. a small percentage of the sewage reaches the plant by means of gravity
    B. all sewage reaches the plant by means of gravity
    C. where sewage cannot reach the plant by gravity it is pumped
    D. pumping is used so that all sewage can reach the plant

17. According to the above paragraph, the reason that some plants are built above the level of the sewerage system is that   17._____

    A. these plants operate more efficiently this way
    B. gravity will naturally bring the sewage in at a lower level
    C. pumping of the sewage is more expensive
    D. these plants are cheaper to build this way

Questions 18-20.

DIRECTIONS: Questions 18 through 20, inclusive, should be answered in accordance with the following paragraph.

Accident proneness is a subject which deserves much move objective and competent study than it has received to date. In discussing accident proneness, it is important to differentiate between the employee who is a "repeater" and one who is truly accident prone. It is obvious that any person put on work of which he knows little without thorough training in safe practice for the work in question will be liable to injury until he does learn the "how" of it. Few workmen left to their own devices will develop adequate safe practices. Therefore, they must be trained. Only those who fail to respond to proper training should be regarded as accident prone. The repeater whose accident record can be explained by a correctible physical defect, by correctible plant or machine hazards, by assignment to work for which he is not suited because of physical deficiencies or special abilities, cannot be fairly called "accident prone."

18. According to the above paragraph, a person is considered accident prone if   18.____

   A. he has accidents regardless of the fact that he has been properly trained
   B. he has many accidents
   C. it is possible for him to have accidents
   D. he works at a job where accidents are possible

19. According to the above paragraph,   19.____

   A. workers will learn the safe way of doing things if left to their own intelligence
   B. most workers must be trained to be safe
   C. a worker who has had more than one accident has not been properly trained
   D. intelligent workers are always safe

20. According to the above paragraph, a person would not be called accident prone if the   20.____
    cause of his accidents was

   A. a lack of interest in the job
   B. recklessness
   C. a low level of intelligence
   D. eyeglasses that don't fit properly

Questions 21-23.

DIRECTIONS: Questions 21 through 23, inclusive, should be answered in accordance with
               the following paragraph.
   Sharpening a twist drill by hand is a skill that is mastered only after much practice and care-ful attention to the details. Therefore, whenever possible, use a tool grinder in which the drills can be properly positioned, clamped in place, and set with precision for the various angles. This machine grinding will enable you to sharpen the drills accurately. As a result, they will last longer and will produce more accurate holes.

21. According to the above paragraph, one reason for sharpening drills accurately is that the   21.____
    drills

   A. can then be used in a hand drill as well as a drill press
   B. will last longer
   C. can then be used by unskilled persons
   D. cost less

22. According to the above paragraph,   22.____

   A. it is easier to sharpen a drill by machine than by hand
   B. drills cannot be sharpened by hand
   C. only a skilled mechanic can learn to sharpen a drill by hand
   D. a good mechanic will learn to sharpen drills by hand

23. As used in the above paragraph, the word *precision* means MOST NEARLY   23.____

   A. accuracy   B. ease   C. rigidity   D. speed

Questions 24-27.

DIRECTIONS: Questions 24 through 27, inclusive, should be answered in accordance with the following paragraph.

Centrifugal pumps have relatively fewer moving parts than reciprocating pumps, and no valves. While reciprocating pumps when new are usually more efficient than centrifugal pumps, the latter retain their efficiency longer. Most rotary pumps are also without valves, but they have closely meshed parts between which high pressures may be set up after they begin to wear. In general, centrifugal pumps can be made much smaller than reciprocating pumps giving the same result. There is an exception, in that positive displacement pumps delivering small volumes at high heads are smaller than equivalent centrifugal pumps. Centrifugal pumps cost less when first purchased than other comparable pumps. The original outlay may be as little as one-third or one-half that of a reciprocating pump suitable for the same purpose.

24. The type of pump NOT mentioned in the above paragraph is the _____ type.   24.____

    A. rotary
    C. reciprocating
    B. propeller
    D. centrifugal

25. According to the above paragraph, the type of pump that sometimes has valves and sometimes does NOT is the   25.____

    A. rotary
    C. reciprocating
    B. propeller
    D. centrifugal

26. According to the above paragraph, centrifugal pumps are   26.____

    A. *always smaller* than reciprocating pumps
    B. *smaller* than reciprocating pumps only when designed to deliver small quantities at low pressures
    C. *larger* than reciprocating pumps only when designed to deliver small quantities at high pressures
    D. *larger* than reciprocating pumps only when designed to deliver large quantities at low pressures

27. The advantage of centrifugal pumps that is NOT mentioned in the above paragraph is that   27.____

    A. the centrifugal pump retains its efficiency longer
    B. it is impossible to create an excessive pressure when using a centrifugal pump
    C. there are fewer parts to wear out in a centifugal pump
    D. the centrifugal pump is cheaper

Questions 28-30.

DIRECTIONS: Questions 28 through 30, inclusive, should be answered in accordance with the following paragraph.

Gaskets made of relatively soft materials are placed between the meeting surfaces of hydraulic fittings in order to increase the tightness of the seal. They should be composed of materials that will not be affected by the liquid to be enclosed, nor by the conditions under which the system operates, including maximum pressure and temperature. They should be able to maintain the amount of clearance required between meeting surfaces. One of the materials most widely used in making gaskets is neoprene. Since neoprene is flexible, it is often used in sheet form at points where a gasket must expand enough to allow air to accumulate, as with cover plates on supply tanks. Over a period of time, oil tends to deteriorate the material used in making neoprene gaskets. The condition of the gasket must, therefore, be checked whenever the unit is disassembled. Since neoprene gasket material is soft and flexible, it easily becomes misshapen, scratched or torn. Great care is, therefore, necessary in handling neoprene. Shellac, gasket sealing compounds or "pipe dope" should never be used with sheet neoprene, unless absolutely necessary for satisfactory installation.

28. Of the following, the one that is NOT mentioned in the above paragraph as a requirement for a good gasket material is that the material must be   28.____

    A. cheap
    B. unaffected by heat developed in a system
    C. relatively soft
    D. capable of maintaining required clearances

29. According to the above paragraph, neoprene will be affected by   29.____

    A. air   B. temperature
    C. pressure   D. oil

30. According to the above paragraph, care is necessary in handling neoprene because   30.____

    A. its condition must be checked frequently
    B. it tears easily
    C. pipe dope should not be used
    D. it is difficult to use

Questions 31-35.

DIRECTIONS: Questions 31 through 35, inclusive, should be answered in accordance with the following statements and instructions.

Column A below lists defects that often happen to equipment that is used in a sewage disposal plant. Column B shows the equipment that is used in such a plant. In the space at the right next to the number of the defect listed in Column A, select the letter in Column B representing the piece of equipment with which this defect is MOST closely associated.

COLUMN A	COLUMN B	
31. Broken shear pin	A. Centrifugal pump	31.____
32. Worn collector ring	B. Wound rotor motor	32.____
33. Pitted impeller	C. Bar screen	33.____
34. Worn chain	D. Methane-gas engine	34.____
35. Crankpin bearing		35.____

36. It is often said that in selecting a man for a job, dependability is more important than seniority. This is because   36._____

    A. it is difficult to judge the amount of work an older man can do
    B. an older man will know how to *avoid* work better
    C. the dependable man is the man you can count on to do the job as called for
    D. the dependable man will require fewer instructions

37. *A man may be conscientious, and yet not be efficient.* This statement MOST likely means that   37._____

    A. a man will not be able to do a job properly unless he has special training
    B. a man may want to do a job well, but may not know how to go about doing it
    C. if a man is efficient, he may not be conscientious
    D. the more conscientious a man is the less efficient he will be

38. If you were a senior sewage treatment worker, a good way of building up the morale of men assigned to you would be to   38._____

    A. overlook minor infractions of the rules
    B. pass the blame for bad assignments to your superiors
    C. treat the men fairly
    D. cover up for men who have made mistakes in their jobs

39. Threatening your subordinates with penalties for neglect of duty is   39._____

    A. *good* practice just to frighten them, even though the penalties will not be inflicted
    B. *poor* practice since men should never be threatened
    C. *good* practice if the penalty is actually going to be inflicted
    D. *poor* practice because men ought to work properly without threats

40. Of the following, the BEST indication that men are dissatisfied with their jobs is that they   40._____

    A. offer suggestions on improving operations
    B. appoint a grievance committee
    C. all join a union
    D. frequently leave for other jobs

41. If a senior sewage treatment worker must reprimand one of the men under him, the reprimand should be given   41._____

    A. in a loud tone of voice so that the man is properly impressed
    B. firmly but quietly
    C. the next day when the senior can get the man alone
    D. in front of the entire crew so that the rest of the men know what is right

42. If a senior sewage treatment worker is not sure of how a job should be done, he should   42._____

    A. make believe he does so that his men will not discover his lack of knowledge
    B. get someone else to do the job
    C. ask his superior how the job should be done
    D. put the job off until he can learn from another crew how it should be done

43. A senior sewage treatment worker makes a mistake, and admits it to his men.   43._____
This practice is _____, because the men _____.

     A. *good;* will respect him more
     B. *poor;* will not trust his judgment anymore
     C. *good;* will then learn to check everything he does before wasting time doing jobs improperly
     D. *poor;* should not know why a job is being done in the way it is

44. A supervisor can BEST earn the respect of his men by   44._____

     A. never criticizing his men
     B. taking the blame for all actions of his men
     C. defending his men from all criticism, regardless of whether the criticism is deserved or not
     D. defending his men from unsupported criticism

45. As a senior sewage treatment worker, you have been ordered by the engineer to do a job   45._____
in a certain manner which you think is not a good way of doing the job. You should

     A. tell the engineer you should be permitted to do the job in whatever way you feel best
     B. avoid doing the job
     C. do the job, but tell your men that you are not responsible for the method being used
     D. explain your objections to the engineer, but then do the job in whatever manner the engineer decides

46. The MOST important requirement for a good supervisor is to have   46._____

     A. physical strength   B. the ability to handle men
     C. manual dexterity   D. good appearance

47. A good senior sewage treatment worker should   47._____

     A. give all the disagreeable assignments to the laziest worker
     B. give all the good assignments to the best worker
     C. give disagreeable assignments to those men who have special training for them
     D. rotate disagreeable assignments among the men

48. A new sewage treatment worker has been assigned to work under you as a senior.   48._____
The MOST important information you should get from the new man is

     A. his age
     B. the type of work he likes to do
     C. his previous experience
     D. how well he gets along with other men

49. A member of your crew, who frequently comes to you with unjustified complaints, comes   49._____
to you again with another complaint.
You should

     A. cut the man short and tell him to stop complaining unnecessarily
     B. listen to the complaint, but do nothing about it
     C. listen to the complaint, and then tell the man the complaint is not justified
     D. check the complaint to see if it is justified

50. To insure that the men working under him are doing their work properly, a senior sewage treatment worker should   50._____

    A. check their work frequently
    B. have the men prepare a written report about the work
    C. assign one individual to be responsible for each job
    D. keep a record of the supplies they use

_____

KEY (CORRECT ANSWERS)

1.	C	11.	D	21.	B	31.	C	41.	B
2.	B	12.	C	22.	A	32.	B	42.	C
3.	C	13.	B	23.	A	33.	A	43.	A
4.	B	14.	C	24.	B	34.	C	44.	D
5.	B	15.	B	25.	A	35.	D	45.	D
6.	D	16.	B	26.	C	36.	C	46.	B
7.	A	17.	D	27.	B	37.	B	47.	D
8.	C	18.	A	28.	A	38.	C	48.	C
9.	D	19.	B	29.	D	39.	C	49.	D
10.	C	20.	D	30.	B	40.	D	50.	A

_____

EXAMINATION SECTION
TEST 1

DIRECTIONS: Each question or incomplete statement is followed by several suggested answers or completions. Select the one that BEST answers the question or completes the statement. *PRINT THE LETTER OF THE CORRECT ANSWER IN THE SPACE AT THE RIGHT.*

1. Reprimanding a crew member before other workers is a   1.____

   A. *good* practice; the reprimand serves as a warning to the other workers
   B. *bad* practice; people usually resent criticism made in public
   C. *good* practice; the other workers will realize that the supervisor is fair
   D. *bad* practice; the other workers will take sides in the dispute

2. Of the following actions, the one which is LEAST likely to promote good work is for the   2.____
   group leader to

   A. praise workers for doing a good job
   B. call attention to the opportunities for promotion for better workers
   C. threaten to recommend discharge of workers who are below standard
   D. put into practice any good suggestion made by crew members

3. A supervisor notices that a member of his crew has skipped a routine oiling of a   3.____
   machine.
   Of the following, the BEST action for the supervisor to take is to

   A. promptly question the worker about the incident
   B. immediately assign another man to oil the machine
   C. bring up the incident the next time the worker asks for a favor
   D. say nothing about the incident but watch the worker carefully in the future

4. Assume you have been told to show a new worker how to operate a piece of equipment.   4.____
   Your FIRST step should be to

   A. ask the worker if he has any questions about the equipment
   B. permit the worker to operate the equipment himself while you carefully watch to
      prevent damage
   C. demonstrate the operation of the equipment for the worker
   D. have the worker read an instruction booklet on the maintenance of the equipment

5. Whenever a new man was assigned to his crew, the supervisor would introduce him to all   5.____
   other crew members, take him on a tour of the plant, tell him about bus schedules and
   places to eat.
   This practice is

   A. *good;* the new man is made to feel welcome
   B. *bad;* supervisors should not interfere in personal matters
   C. *good;* the new man knows that he can bring his personal problems to the supervi-
      sor
   D. *bad;* work time should not be spent on personal matters

6. The MOST important factor in successful leadership is the ability to   6._____

    A. obtain instant obedience to all orders
    B. establish friendly personal relations with crew members
    C. avoid disciplining crew members
    D. make crew members want to do what should be done

7. Explaining the reasons for departmental procedure to workers tends to   7._____

    A. waste time which should be used for productive purposes
    B. increase their interest in their work
    C. make them more critical of departmental procedures
    D. confuse them

8. If you want a job done well, do it yourself.   8._____
For a supervisor to following this advice would be

    A. *good;* a supervisor is responsible for the work of his crew
    B. *bad;* a supervisor should train his men, not do their work
    C. *good;* a supervisor should be skilled in all jobs assigned to his cre
    D. *bad;* a supervisor loses respect when he works with his hands

9. When a supervisor discovers a mistake in one of the jobs for which his crew is responsi-   9._____
ble, it is MOST important for him to find out

    A. whether anybody else knows about the mistake
    B. who was to blame for the mistake
    C. how to prevent similar mistakes in the future
    D. whether similar mistakes occurred in the past

10. A supervisor who has to explain a new procedure to his crew should realize that ques-   10._____
tions from the crew usually show that they

    A. are opposed to the new procedure
    B. are completely confused by the explanation
    C. need more training in the new procedure
    D. are interested in the explanation

11. A supervisor assigns one of his crew to sweep the area around the trash racks. A short   11._____
time later, the supervisor notices that the trash rack area has not been swept. Of the following, the BEST way for the supervisor to handle this is to

    A. ask the crew member why he has not swept the area
    B. reprimand the crew member for not obeying orders
    C. assign another crew member to sweep the area
    D. sweep the area himself

12. Suppose that a member of your crew complains that you are *playing favorites* in assign-   12._____
ing work.
Of the following, the BEST method of handling the complaint is to

    A. deny it and refuse to discuss the matter with the worker
    B. take the opportunity to tell the worker what is wrong with his work

C. ask the worker for examples to prove his point and try to clear up any misunder-
standing
D. promise to be more careful in making assignments in the future

13. A member of your crew comes to you with a complaint. After discussing the matter with
him, it is clear that you have convinced him that his complaint was not justified.
At this point, you should

A. permit him to drop the matter
B. make him admit his error
C. pretend to see some justification in his complaint
D. warn him against making unjustified complaints

14. Suppose that a supervisor has in his crew an older man who works rather slowly. In other
respects, this man is a good worker; he is seldom absent, works carefully, never loafs,
and is cooperative.
The BEST way for the supervisor to handle this worker is to

A. try to get him to work faster and less carefully
B. give him the most disagreeable jobs
C. request that he be given special training
D. permit him to work at his own speed

15. Suppose that a member of your crew comes to you with a suggestion he thinks will save
time in doing a job. You realize immediately that it won't work.
Under these circumstances, your BEST action would be to

A. thank the worker for the suggestion and forget about it
B. explain to the worker why you think it won't work
C. tell the worker to put the suggestion in writing
D. ask the other members of your crew to criticize the suggestion

Questions 16-18.

DIRECTIONS: Questions 16 through 18 are to be answered on the basis of the following
paragraph.

*Thermostats should be tested in hot water for proper opening. A bucket should be filled
with sufficient water to cover the thermostat and fitted with a thermometer suspended in the
water so that the sensitive bulb portion does not rest directly on the bucket. The water is then
heated on a stove. As the temperature of the water passes the 160-165° range, the thermostat should start to open and should be completely opened when the temperature has risen to
185-190°. Lifting the thermostat into the air should cause a pronounced closing action, and
the unit should be closed entirely within a short time.*

16. The thermostat described above is a device which opens and closes with changes in the

A. position
C. temperature
B. pressure
D. surroundings

17. According to the above paragraph, the closing action of the thermostat should be tested   17.____
by

    A. working the thermostat back and forth
    B. permitting the water to cool gradually
    C. adding cold water to the bucket
    D. removing the thermostat from the bucket

18. The bulb of the thermometer should NOT rest directly on the bucket because   18.____

    A. the bucket gets hotter than the water
    B. the thermometer might be damaged in that position
    C. it is difficult to read the thermometer in that position
    D. the thermometer might interfere with operation of the thermostat

Questions 19-21.

DIRECTIONS: Questions 19 through 21 are to be answered on the basis of the following paragraph.

All idle pumps should be turned daily by hand, and should be run under power at least once a week. Whenever repairs are made on a pump, a record should be kept so that it will be possible to judge the success with which the pump is performing its functions. If a pump fails to deliver liquid, there may be an obstruction in the suction line, the pump's parts may be badly worn, or the packing defective.

19. According to the above paragraph, pumps   19.____

    A. in use should be turned by hand every day
    B. which are not in use should be run under power every day
    C. which are in daily use should be run under power several times a week
    D. which are not in use should be turned by hand every day

20. According to the above paragraph, the reason for keeping records of repairs made on   20.____
pumps is to

    A. make certain that proper maintenance is being performed
    B. discover who is responsible for improper repairs
    C. rate the performance of the pumps
    D. know when to replace worn parts

21. The one of the following causes of pump failure which is NOT mentioned in the above   21.____
paragraph is

    A. excessive suction lift   B. clogged lines
    C. bad packing   D. worn parts

Questions 22-24.

DIRECTIONS: Questions 22 through 24 are to be answered on the basis of the following
paragraph.

*The bearings of all electrical equipment should be subjected to careful inspection at
scheduled periodic intervals in order to secure maximum life. The newer type of sleeve bearings requires very little attention since the oil does not become contaminated and oil leakage
is negligible. Maintenance of the correct oil level is frequently the only upkeep required for
years of service with this type of bearing.*

22.   According to the above paragraph, the MAIN reason for making periodic inspections of   22.____
      electrical equipment is to

      A.   reduce waste of lubricants
      B.   prevent injury to operators
      C.   make equipment last longer
      D.   keep operators *on their toes*

23.   According to the above paragraph, the bearings of electrical equipment should be   23.____
      inspected

      A.   whenever the equipment isn't working properly
      B.   whenever there is time for inspections
      C.   at least once a year
      D.   at regular times

24.   According to the above paragraph, when using newer type of sleeve bearings,   24.____

      A.   oil leakage is slight
      B.   the oil level should be checked every few years
      C.   oil leakage is due to carelessness
      D.   oil soon becomes dirty

25.   The MAIN reason for treating sewage before emptying it into the ocean is to   25.____

      A.   prevent pollution of the water
      B.   remove disagreeable odors
      C.   protect fishing areas
      D.   obtain valuable by-products

_____

KEY (CORRECT ANSWERS)

1.	B		11.	A
2.	C		12.	C
3.	A		13.	A
4.	C		14.	D
5.	A		15.	B
6.	D		16.	C
7.	B		17.	D
8.	B		18.	A
9.	C		19.	D
10.	D		20.	C

21. A
22. C
23. D
24. A
25. A

TEST 2

DIRECTIONS: Each question or incomplete statement is followed by several suggested answers or completions. Select the one that BEST answers the question or completes the statement. *PRINT THE LETTER OF THE CORRECT ANSWER IN THE SPACE AT THE RIGHT.*

Questions 1-3.

DIRECTIONS: Questions 1 through 3, inclusive, are to be answered in accordance with the information given in the paragraph below.

The soda-acid fire extinguisher is the commonest type of water solution extinguisher in which pressure is used to expel the water. The chemicals used are sodium bicarbonate (baking soda) and sulfuric acid. The sodium bicarbonate is dissolved in water, and this solution is the extinguishing agent. The extinguishing, value of the stream is that of an equal quantity of water.

1. According to the above paragraph, the soda-acid extinguisher, compared to others of the same type, is the
1.____

    A. most widely used
    B. most effective in putting out fire
    C. cheapest to operate
    D. easiest to operate

2. In the soda-acid extinguisher, the fire is put out by a solution of sodium bicarbonate and
2.____

    A. sulfuric acid   B. baking soda
    C. soda-acid   D. water

3. According to the above paragraph, the sodium bicarbonate solution, compared to water, is
3.____

    A. *more* effective in putting out fires
    B. *less* effective in putting out fires
    C. *equally* effective in putting out fires
    D. *more or less* effective, depending upon the type of fire

Questions 4-6.

DIRECTIONS: Questions 4 through 6, inclusive, are to be answered in accordance with the information given in the paragraph below.

Some gases which may be inhaled have an irritant effect on the respiratory tract. Among them are ammonia fumes, hydrogen sulfide, nitrous fumes, and phosgene. Persons who have been exposed to irritant gases must lie down at once and keep absolutely quiet until the doctor arrives. The action of some of these gases may be delayed, and at first the victim may show few or no symptoms.

4. According to the above paragraph, the part of the body that is most affected by irritant gases is the   4._____

   A. heart   B. lungs   C. skin   D. nerves

5. According to the above paragraph, a person who has inhaled an irritant gas should be   5._____

   A. given artificial respiration
   B. made to rest
   C. wrapped in blankets
   D. made to breathe smelling salts

6. A person is believed to have come in contact with an irritant gas but he does not become sick immediately. According to the above paragraph, we may conclude that the person   6._____

   A. did not really come in contact with the gas
   B. will become sick later
   C. came in contact with a small amount of gas
   D. may possibly become sick later

7. The BEST way for a supervisor to reduce the number of accidents among his workers is to   7._____

   A. draw up detailed safety procedures
   B. constantly inspect the operation for dangerous practices
   C. carefully investigate the cause of every accident
   D. develop safety consciousness in his workers

8. The MAIN reason for enclosing switches and other current-carrying parts of electrical systems is to   8._____

   A. exclude dirt and moisture
   B. protect workers from shock
   C. increase the capacity of the equipment
   D. prevent damage to the equipment

9. Sewage treatment workers who work near electrical equipment should avoid touching wires particularly when wearing   9._____

   A. rubber-soled shoes   B. wet clothing
   C. loose-fitting clothing   D. nylon clothing

10. A leak in a chlorine tank is dangerous because chlorine   10._____

   A. may cause an explosion   B. may corrode equipment
   C. is an irritating gas   D. is highly flammable

11. Suppose that a member of your crew falls down a flight of stairs and severely injures his leg.
    While waiting for the doctor, you should try to   11._____

   A. make the injured man comfortable and prevent further injury
   B. put a splint on his leg if it appears to be broken
   C. question the injured man about the cause of the accident
   D. exercise the injured leg to prevent muscle tightening

12. Suppose that you see some acid splash into the eyes of a fellow worker. 12._____
The one of the following actions that you should take FIRST is to

    A. bandage his eyes with a clean dressing
    B. place boric acid ointment in his eyes
    C. make him lie down and close his eyes
    D. wash his eyes with large amounts of clean water

13. Suppose that you discover an unconscious man who has fallen across a *live* electric 13._____
wire.
Of the following, the action that you should take FIRST is to

    A. break the contact between the man and the live wire
    B. give the man artificial respiration
    C. loosen the man's clothing and treat him for shock
    D. apply sterile dressings to the man's burns

14. It is important to know the location of pressure points when treating persons suffering 14._____
from

    A. shock   B. bleeding   C. poisoning   D. burns

15. The one of the following diseases which may be caused by the pollution of drinking water 15._____
by sewage is

    A. malaria   B. typhoid fever
    C. tuberculosis   D. muscular dystrophy

16. The one of the following gases which is a valuable byproduct of the treatment of sewage 16._____
is

    A. methane   B. chlorine
    C. hydrogen sulfide   D. ammonia

17. In the city sewage system, MOST digested sludge is 17._____

    A. used as soil fertilizer   B. dumped into the ocean
    C. used as land fill   D. processed into soap

18. The MAIN reason for painting metal equipment in a sewage plant is to 18._____

    A. cut down on repairs and replacement of equipment
    B. improve the appearance of the plant
    C. make it easier to inspect the equipment
    D. eliminate the need for cleaning the equipment

19. A pump is able to fill a tank holding 15,000 gallons in 2 hours and 30 minutes. Pumping 19._____
at the same rate, an empty 60,000 gallon tank can be filled in _____ hours.

    A. 10   B. 10/1/2   C. 11   D. 11 1/2

20. Assume you want to add 10,000 gallons of water to a tank. If you pump water into the 20._____
tank at the rate of 100 gallons per minute for one hour and 50 gallons per minute after
the first hour, the total time required to add the 10,000 gallons is MOST NEARLY

    A. 1 hour and 20 minutes   B. 2 hours
    C. 2 hours and 20 minutes   D. 3 hours

4 (#2)

21. A tank 25 feet long, 15 feet wide, and 10 feet deep is enlarged by extending the length   21.____
    another 25 feet.
    The enlarged tank will be able to hold _____ more than the original tank.

    A. 50%   B. 100%   C. 150%   D. 200%

Questions 22-24.

DIRECTIONS: Questions 22 through 24, inclusive, are to be answered in accordance with the
              information given below.

    At midnight of each day, readings are made of gas consumption meters. Readings for 8
days are as follows:

Sunday	6873 cu.ft.	Thursday	3246 cu.ft.
Monday	8147 cu.ft.	Friday	4962 cu.ft.
Tuesday	0065 cu.ft.	Saturday	6823 cu.ft.
Wednesday	1480 cu.ft.	Sunday	7179 cu.ft.

22. According to the above table, the total gas consumed for the week was MOST NEARLY   22.____
    _____ cu.ft.

    A. 1000   B. 4000   C. 7000   D. 10,000

23. Gas consumption for Tuesday was MOST NEARLY _____ cu.ft.   23.____

    A. 500   B. 1000   C. 2000   D. 8000

24. The day on which gas consumption was LOWEST was   24.____

    A. Monday   B. Tuesday   C. Wednesday   D. Thursday

25. The yearly summer survey of harbor pollution is made by the department of   25.____

    A. health   B. marine and aviation
    C. public works   D. sanitation

KEY (CORRECT ANSWERS)

1.	A		11.	A
2.	D		12.	D
3.	C		13.	A
4.	B		14.	B
5.	B		15.	B
6.	D		16.	A
7.	D		17.	B
8.	B		18.	A
9.	B		19.	A
10.	C		20.	C

21.	B
22.	D
23.	C
24.	A
25.	C

WORK SCHEDULING
EXAMINATION SECTION
TEST 1

DIRECTIONS: Each question or incomplete statement is followed by several suggested answers or completions. Select the one that BEST answers the question or completes the statement. *PRINT THE LETTER OF THE CORRECT ANSWER IN THE SPACE AT THE RIGHT.*

Questions 1-8.

DIRECTIONS: Questions 1 through 8 are to be answered on the basis of the following information.

Assume that you are the supervisor of a unit that works seven days a week. You need to determine the work and vacation schedules of the employees you supervise for the month of July.

THE EMPLOYEES

Alan W.	9 years seniority	computer operator
Jane B.	4 1/2 years seniority	typist
Alex H.	5 years seniority	security staff
Tony E.	4 years seniority	security staff
Andre T.	4 2/3 years seniority	typist
Mary W.	11 years seniority	security staff
Andy R.	13 years seniority	computer operator
Rhonda L.	2 years seniority	computer operator
Ethel R.	15 years seniority	typist
Roger G.	3 years seniority	security staff

THE VACATION PREFERENCES OF THE EMPLOYEES:

	1st vacation day	1ast vacation day
Alan W.	7/1	7/19
Jane B.	7/15	7/29
Alex H.	7/8	7/22
Tony E.	7/22	7/30
Andre T.	7/1	7/14
Mary W.	7/1	7/22
Andy R.	7/15	7/30
Rhonda L.	7/20	7/31
Ethel R.	7/1	7/27
Roger G.	7/21	7/31

IMPORTANT REGULATIONS REGARDING VACATION LEAVE

Employees with seniority have first choice for their preferred vacation dates. Seniority should be calculated separately for each of the three occupational groups.

There must be two security employees on duty each working day in July. This overrides any other considerations.

There must be one typist on duty each working day in July. This overrides any other considerations.

Employees with least seniority, when denied their first choice of vacation dates, should automatically be scheduled ahead for vacation on the very next date closest to the dates they had originally preferred and the length of the vacation extended the appropriate number of days. Example: A vacation originally requested for 7/13, but changed because of seniority, would be moved AHEAD to a date after 7/13 (to 7/16, for example).

You may want to use the calendar below to help you organize this information.

JULY

1	2	3	4	5	6	7
8	9	10	11	12	13	14
15	16	17	18	19	20	21
22	23	24	25	26	27	28
29	30	31				

1. The number of employees on vacation on July 16 should be   1._____

    A. four   B. five   C. six   D. seven

2. The number of employees on vacation on July 22 should be   2._____

    A. five   B. six   C. seven   D. eight

3. How many typists will be working on July 15?   3._____

    A. One   B. Two   C. Three   D. None

4. How many workers will be on vacation on July 31?   4._____

    A. Two   B. Three   C. Four   D. Five

5. Which of the following is TRUE of the employees in the unit?   5._____
      I.   Andy R., Jane B., Tony E., and Mary W. will be on vacation on 7/22.
      II. Ethel R., Andre T., Mary W., and Alex H. will be on vacation on 7/8.

III. Rhonda L., Tony E., and Roger G. will be on vacation on 7/31, 5.____
IV. Andy R., Jane B., and Ethel R. will be on vacation on 7/28.
THE CORRECT ANSWER IS:

A. I, II, III   B. I, II
C. II, III   D. II

6. How many typists will be working on July 28? 6.____

A. One   B. Two   C. Three   D. Four

7. How many computer operators will be working on July 23? 7.____

A. One   B. Two   C. Three   D. Four

8. Roger G. will begin his vacation on July 8.____

A. 21   B. 22   C. 23   D. 24

Questions 9-15.

DIRECTIONS: Questions 9 through 15 are to be answered on the basis of the following information.

Assume that you are the supervisor of a unit that works seven days a week. You need to
determine the work and vacation schedules of the employees you supervise for the month of
August.

THE EMPLOYEES

	Years Seniority	Position
Robert L.	7	Security staff
Ann N.	71/2	Computer operator
Thomas B.	9	Typist
Phyllis P.	11	Computer operator
Mike D.	3	Security staff
Jane R.	2	Security staff
Alan R.	8	Computer operator
Susan T.	10	Typist
George W.	6	Computer operator
Barbara L.	4	Typist
Jack B.	13	Security staff
Grace N.	12	Typist

THE VACATION PREFERENCES OF THE EMPLOYEES

	1st vacation day	last vacation day
Robert L.	8/3	8/18
Ann N.	8/17	8/28
Thomas B.	8/19	8/28
Phyllis P.	8/5	8/20
Mike D.	8/14	8/21
Jane R.	8/20	8/27
Alan R.	8/12	8/26
Susan T.	8/5	8/26
George W.	8/3	8/14
Barbara L.	8/7	8/21
Jack B.	8/10	8/18
Grace N.	8/4	8/25

IMPORTANT REGULATIONS REGARDING VACATION LEAVE.

Employees with seniority have first choice for their preferred vacation dates. Seniority should be calculated separately for each of the three occupational groups.

There must be two security employees on duty each working day in August. This overrides any other considerations.

There must be two typists on duty from 8/11 to 8/18. This overrides any other considerations.

There must be two computer operators on duty each working day in August. This overrides any other considerations.

Employees with least seniority, when denied their first choice of vacation dates, should automatically be scheduled ahead for their vacation on the very next date closest to the date they originally preferred, and the length of the vacation extended the appropriate number of days. Example: A vacation originally requested for 8/18, but changed because of seniority, would be moved AHEAD to a date after 8/18 (to 8/21, for example).

You may wish to use the calendar on the next page to help you organize this information.

AUGUST

1	2	3	4	5	6	7
8	9	10	11	12	13	14
15	16	17	18	19	20	21
22	23	24	25	26	27	28
29	30	31				

9. How many workers will be on vacation on August 21? 9._____

    A. Five   B. Six   C. Seven   D. Eight

10. How many workers will be working on August 28? 10._____

    A. Six   B. Seven   C. Eight   D. Nine

11. Of the following, who will NOT work on August 27?   11.____

    A. Alan R.   B. George W.   C. Mike D.   D. Susan T.

12. Of the following, who will work on August 19?   12.____

    A. Thomas B.   B. Barbara L.
    C. Ann N.   D. Mike D.

13. How many typists will be on vacation on August 19?   13.____

    A. One   B. Two   C. Three   D. Four

14. How many workers will be on vacation on August 17?   14.____

    A. Five   B. Six   C. Eight   D. Nine

15. How many workers will work on August 11?   15.____

    A. Seven   B. Eight   C. Five   D. Six

———

KEY (CORRECT ANSWERS)

1.	C	6.	B	11.	B
2.	B	7.	A	12.	C
3.	A	8.	C	13.	D
4.	B	9.	D	14.	B
5.	C	10.	C	15.	A

———

EXAMINATION SECTION
TEST 1

DIRECTIONS: Each question or incomplete statement is followed by several suggested answers or completions. Select the one that BEST answers the question or completes the statement. *PRINT THE LETTER OF THE CORRECT ANSWER IN THE SPACE AT THE RIGHT.*

1. The MAJOR responsibility of a director is to   1.____

    A. make certain that his line supervisors keep proper control of staff activity
    B. see that training is given to his staff according to individual needs
    C. insure that his total organization is coordinated toward agency goals and objectives
    D. work constructively with groups so that programs will reflect their needs

2. A good organization chart of a department is an IMPORTANT instrument because it can   2.____

    A. make it easier to understand the mission of the department
    B. help new employees become acquainted with department personnel
    C. clarify relationships and responsibilities of the various department components
    D. simplify the task of *going to the top*

3. Unnecessary and obsolete forms can be eliminated MOST effectively by   3.____

    A. appointing a representative committee to review and evaluate all forms in relation to operating procedures
    B. discarding all forms which have not been used during the past year
    C. assembling all forms and destroying those which are duplicates or obsolete
    D. directing office managers to review the forms to determine which should be revised or abolished

4. The director must adopt methods and techniques to insure that his budgeted allowances are properly spent and that organizational objectives are being reached.
These responsibilities can be fulfilled BEST by   4.____

    A. controlling operations with electronic data processing equipment
    B. shifting caseload controls from caseworkers to clerical staff
    C. installing a work simplification program and establishing controls for crucial areas of operation
    D. assigning employees with special skills and training to perform the more important and specialized jobs

5. The MOST appropriate technique for making the staff thoroughly familiar with departmental policies would be to   5.____

    A. maintain an up-to-date loose-leaf binder of written policies in a central point in the office
    B. issue copies of all policy directives to the unit supervisors
    C. distribute copies of policy directives to the entire staff and arrange for follow-up discussion on a unit basis
    D. discuss all major policy directives at an office-wide staff meeting

6. When a proposed change in a departmental procedure is being evaluated, the factor which should be considered MOST important in reaching the decision is the

    A. extent of resistance anticipated from members of the staff
    B. personnel needed to execute the proposed change
    C. time required for training staff in the revised procedure
    D. degree of organizational dislocation compared with gains expected from the change

6.____

7. A director anticipates that certain aspects of a new departmental procedure will be distasteful to many staff members.
    Assuming that the procedure is basically sound in spite of this drawback, the BEST approach for the director to take with his staff is to

    A. advise them to accept the procedure since it has the support of the highest authorities in the department
    B. point out that other procedures which were resisted initially have come to be accepted in time
    C. challenge staff members to suggest another procedure which will accomplish the same purpose better
    D. ask the staff members to discuss the *pros* and *cons* of the procedure and suggest how it can be improved

7.____

8. At a staff meeting at which a basic change in departmental procedure is to be announced, a director begins the discussion by asking the participants for criticisms of the existing procedure. He then describes the new procedure to be employed and explains the improvements that are anticipated.
    The director's method of introducing the change is

    A. *good,* mainly because the participants would be more receptive to the new procedure if they understood the inadequacies of the old one
    B. *good,* mainly because the participants' comments on the old procedure will provide the basis for evaluation of the feasibility of the new one
    C. *bad,* mainly because the participants will realize that the decision for change has been made before the meeting, without consideration of the participants' comments
    D. *bad,* mainly because the discussion is focused on the old procedure, rather than on the procedure being introduced

8.____

9. Assume that you are conducting a staff conference to discuss the development of a procedure implementing a change in state policy. There are twelve participants whose office titles range from unit supervisor to senior supervisor, each of whom has responsibility for some aspect of the program affected by the policy change. After some introductory remarks, the BEST procedure for you to follow is to call upon the participants in the order of their

    A. titles, with the highest titles first because they are likely to have the most experience and knowledge of the subject
    B. titles, with the lower titles first because they are likely to be less inhibited if they are permitted to give their views before the senior participants speak
    C. places around the table, to promote informality and democratic procedure
    D. specialized knowledge of the subject so that those with the most knowledge and competence may lead the discussion

9.____

10. A staff member has suggested a way of reducing the time required to prepare a monthly report by combining several items of information, separating one item into two parts, and generally revising definitions of terms.
The CHIEF disadvantage of such a revision is that

    A. comparison of present with past periods will be more difficult
    B. subordinates who prepare the report will require retraining
    C. forms currently in use will have to be discarded
    D. employees using the records will be confused by the changes

10.____

11. Assume that a director happens to be present at a regular staff conference conducted by a senior supervisor. During the course of the conference, the director frequently takes over the discussion in order to amplify remarks made by the supervisor, to impart information about departmental policies, and to modify or correct possible misinterpretations of the supervisor's remarks.
The director's actions in this situation are

    A. *proper,* mainly because the conference members were given the latest and most accurate information concerning departmental policies
    B. *proper,* mainly because the director has an obligation to assist and support the supervisor
    C. *improper,* mainly because the director did not completely take over the conference
    D. *improper,* mainly because the supervisor was put in a difficult position in the presence of his staff

11.____

12. A center has a serious staff morale problem because of rumors that it will probably be abolished. To handle this situation, the director adopts a policy of promptly corroborating rumors that he knows to be true and denying false ones.
Although this method of dealing with the situation should have some good results, its CHIEF weakness is that

    A. it *chases* the rumors instead of forestalling them by giving correct information concerning the center's future
    B. the director may not have the necessary information at hand
    C. status is given to the rumors as a result of the attention paid to them
    D. the director may inadvertently divulge confidential information

12.____

13. Realizing the importance of harmonious staff relationships, one of your supervisors makes a practice of unobtrusively intervening in any conflict situation among staff members. Whenever friction seems to be developing, he attempts to soothe ruffled feelings and remove the source of difficulty by such methods as rescheduling, reassigning personnel, etc. His efforts are always behind the scenes and unknown to the personnel involved.
This practice may produce some good results, but the CHIEF drawback is that it

    A. permits staff to engage in unacceptable practices without correction
    B. violates the principle of chain of command
    C. involves the supervisor in personal relationships which are not properly his concern
    D. requires confidential sources of information about personal relationships within the center

13.____

14. Assume that the department adopts a policy of transferring administrative personnel   14._____
from one center to another after stated periods of service in a center, or in a central office.
Of the following, the MAIN advantage of such a policy is that it helps

   A. prevent the formation of cliques among staff members
   B. key staff members keep abreast of new developments
   C. effect a greater utilization of staff members' special talents
   D. develop a broader outlook and loyalty to the department as a whole, rather than to
   one center

15. A delegation of union members meets with you in your role as director to discuss obtain-   15._____
ing assistance for a group of strikers who live in the neighborhood covered by the center.
In the course of discussion, you learn that the strike has been called by the local union
against the explicit directive of the national union's leadership.
The MOST appropriate course of action for you to take in this instance is to advise the
union committee

   A. of your sympathy and assure them that individual applications from the strikers for
   assistance will receive priority
   B. that if the strikers are in need, they will be able to receive assistance as long as
   they are on strike
   C. that since the strike is illegal, none of the workers will be eligible for assistance
   D. that there is no bar to any of the strikers receiving assistance provided they are in
   need and are ready and willing to accept other employment if offered

16. The quality control system is a management tool used to test the validity of the eligibility   16._____
caseload.
This system can be helpful to a director in the following ways, with the EXCEPTION of

   A. obtaining objective data to use in evaluating the performance of specific staff mem-
   bers
   B. identifying the need for policy changes
   C. sorting out the source of errors in determining eligibility
   D. setting up training objectives for his staff

17. As director, you observe that there has been a sharp rise in the number of fair hearings,   17._____
The increase seems to coincide with the intensified activities of the local recipients' orga-
nization.
The MOST appropriate action under the circumstances is to

   A. determine whether the fair hearing requests result from weaknesses in the center's
   operation, and remedy the causes, if feasible
   B. disregard the matter for the time being because complaints have been stirred up by
   an organized client group
   C. emphasize to your staff the importance of meeting client needs promptly in order to
   avoid fair hearing requests
   D. resolve the grievances with the leaders of the recipients' organization

18. As director, you receive notice of a fair hearing decision from the State Commissioner   18.____
ordering you to restore assistance to a family. You are appalled by the order because the
facts cited by the hearing officer are at complete variance with what actually occurred,
according to your personal knowledge of the case.
Of the following, the MOST appropriate course of action for you to take first is to

    A. point out to central office that the decision should be reconsidered and appropri-
ately modified
    B. comply with the decision under protest because it is patently wrong
    C. recommend to central office that it consider court action through an Article 78 pro-
ceeding to correct the erroneous decision
    D. comply with the decision, although an order of the State Commissioner has no
force and effect of law

19. In your capacity as director, you have received a copy of the monthly statistical report   19.____
issued by the department. In reviewing the report, you note that your center is showing a
rise in caseload which is substantially higher than the average rise throughout the city.
Which of the alternatives listed below would be MOST appropriate in order to deal with
this situation?

    A. Make plans to discuss the situation with central office so that appropriate corrective
action can be taken on the basis of your consultation
    B. Collect necessary information and data about the operations of your center and the
area it serves to determine the cause of the trend, and plan appropriate action on
the basis of your findings
    C. Call a meeting of your unit supervisors in order to impress upon them the impor-
tance of more diligent efforts to assist clients
    D. Assume that the rise in caseload is an inevitable result of the substantial increase
in unemployment, and take no immediate action

20. Of the following phases of a training program for administrative personnel, the one which   20.____
is usually the MOST difficult to formulate is the

    A. selection of training methods for the program
    B. obtaining of frank opinions of the participants as to the usefulness of the program
    C. chief executive officer's judgment as to the need for such a program
    D. evaluation of the effectiveness of the program

21. Assume that you are conducting a conference dealing with problems of the center of   21.____
which you are the director. The problem being discussed is one with which you have had
no experience. However, two of the participants, who have had considerable experience
with it, carry on an extended discussion, showing that they understand the problem thoroughly. The others are very much interested in the discussion and are taking notes on
the material presented. To permit the two staff members to continue for the length of time
allowed for discussion of the problem is

    A. *desirable,* chiefly because introduction of the material by the two participants them-
selves may encourage others to contribute their work experience
    B. *desirable,* chiefly because their discussion may be more meaningful to the others
than a discussion which is not based on work experience
    C. *undesirable,* chiefly because they are discussing material only in light of their own
experience rather than in general terms
    D. *undesirable,* chiefly because it would reveal your own lack of experience with the
problem and undermine your authority with the staff

22. In dealing with staff members, it is a commonly accepted principle that individual differ-   22.____
ences exist, suggesting that employees should be treated in an unlike manner in order to
achieve maximum results from their work assignments.
This statement means MOST NEARLY that

    A. supervisors should be aware of the personal problems of their subordinates and
make allowances for poor performance because of such problems
    B. standardized work rules are ineffective because of the different capabilities of
employees to maintain such work rules
    C. employees' individual needs should be considered by their supervisors to the
greatest extent possible, within the practical limitations of the work situation
    D. knowledge of general principles of human behavior is generally of little use to a
supervisor in assisting him to supervise his subordinates effectively

23. A supervisor under your jurisdiction reports to you that one of his subordinates has been   23.____
taking unusually long lunch hours, has been absent from work frequently, and has been
doing poorer work than previously.
The BEST procedure for you to follow FIRST is to advise the supervisor to

    A. prefer charges against the employee
    B. arrange for a psychological consultation for the employee
    C. ascertain whether the employee is ill and, if so, arrange a medical examination for
him
    D. have a private conversation with the employee to obtain more information about
the reasons for his behavior

24. If the term *executive development* is defined as the continuous, on-going, on-the-job pro-   24.____
cess of constructing plans to improve individuals in specific positions, both for the purpose of present improvement as well as for any future advancement which is envisaged
for the employee, it follows that the emphasis in an executive development program
should

    A. provide learning experiences through formal or informal classes, seminars, or con-
ferences,for which the focus is on the function of the position
    B. be oriented to the individual participant and may include a host of planned activi-
ties, such as appraisal, coaching, counseling, and job rotation
    C. attempt to create needs, to awaken, enlarge, and stimulate the individual so as to
broaden his outlook and potentialities as a human being
    D. insure that the individual is able to plan, organize, direct, and control operations in
the bureau, division, or agency

25. Most psychologists agree that employees have a need for recognition for the work they   25.____
perform. Therefore, it can be concluded that

    A. employees should be praised every time they complete a job satisfactorily
    B. praise is a more effective incentive to good performance than is punishment
    C. administrative personnel should be aware that subordinates do not have needs
similar to their own
    D. a formalized system of rewards and punishment is better than no system at all, as
long as there is a built-in consistency in its administration

KEY (CORRECT ANSWERS)

1.	C	11.	D
2.	C	12.	A
3.	A	13.	A
4.	C	14.	D
5.	C	15.	D
6.	D	16.	A
7.	D	17.	A
8.	C	18.	A
9.	D	19.	B
10.	A	20.	D

21.	B
22.	C
23.	D
24.	B
25.	B

TEST 2

DIRECTIONS: Each question or incomplete statement is followed by several suggested answers or completions. Select the one that BEST answers the question or completes the statement. *PRINT THE LETTER OF THE CORRECT ANSWER IN THE SPACE AT THE RIGHT.*

1. Studies have shown that the MOST effective kind of safety training program is one in which the

   A. training is conducted by consultants who are expert in the nature of the work performed
   B. lectures are given by the top executives in an agency
   C. employees participate in all phases of the program
   D. supervisors are responsible for the safety training

   1.____

2. Of the following, the MOST effective method of selecting potential top executives would be

   A. situational testing which simulates actual conditions
   B. a written test which covers the knowledge required to perform the job
   C. an oral test which requires candidate to discuss significant aspects of the job
   D. a confidential interview with his former employee

   2.____

3. With regard to staff morale, MOST evidence shows that

   A. employees with positive job attitudes always outproduce those with negative job attitudes
   B. morale always relates to the employee's attitude toward his working conditions and his job
   C. low morale always results in poor job performance
   D. high morale has a direct relationship to effective union leadership

   3.____

4. Of the following groups of factors, the group which has been shown to be related to the incidence of job accidents is

   A. personality characteristics, intelligence, defective vision
   B. experience, fatigue, motor and perceptual speed
   C. coordination, fatigue, intelligence
   D. defective vision, motor and perceptual speed, intelligence

   4.____

5. Executives who have difficulty making decisions when faced with a number of choices USUALLY

   A. have domestic problems which interfere with the decision-making process
   B. can be trained to improve their ability to make decisions
   C. are production-oriented rather than employee-centered
   D. do not know their jobs well enough to act decisively

   5.____

6. Studies of disciplinary dismissals of workers reveal that

   A. the majority of employees were dismissed because of lack of technical competence
   B. the supervisors were unusually demanding of employee competence
   C. most employees were dismissed because of inability to work with their co-workers
   D. the chief executive set unrealistic standards of performance

   6.____

7. One philosophy of assigning workers to a specific job is that the worker and his job are   7._____
an integral unit.
This means, MOST NEARLY, that the

    A. employee and the job may both require adjustment
    B. employee must meet all the specifications of the job as a prerequisite for employ-ment
    C. employee's morale will be affected by his salary
    D. employee's job satisfaction has a direct effect on his emotional health

8. The statement that the supervisor and the administrator are the *primary personnel men*   8._____
means, MOST NEARLY, that

    A. supervisors and administrators are more skilled in personnel techniques than are professional personnel technicians
    B. they are in the best position to implement personnel policies and procedures
    C. employees have more confidence in their supervisors and administrators than in the professional personnel administrator
    D. personnel administration is most effective when it combines both centralized and decentralized approaches

9. Administrators frequently have to interview people in order to obtain information.   9._____
Although the interview is a legitimate fact-gathering technique, it has limitations which
should not be overlooked.
The one of the following which is an IMPORTANT limitation is that

    A. individuals generally hesitate to give information orally which they would usually answer in writing
    B. the material derived from the interview can usually be obtained at lower cost from existing records
    C. the emotional attitudes of individuals during an interview often affect the accuracy of the information given
    D. the interview is a poor technique for discovering how well clients understand departmental policies

10. Leadership styles have frequently been categorized as authoritarian, laissez-faire, and   10._____
democratic.
In general, management's reliance on leadership to produce desired results would be
MOST effectively implemented through

    A. the laissez-faire approach when group results are desired
    B. the authoritarian approach in a benevolent manner when quick decisions are required
    C. the democratic approach, when quick decisions are unimportant
    D. all three approaches, depending upon circumstances

11. As director, you are responsible for enforcing a recently established regulation which has   11._____
    aroused antagonism among many clients.
    You should deal with this situation by

    A. explaining to the clients that you are not responsible for making regulations
    B. enforcing the regulation but reporting to your superior the number and kind of com-
        plaints against it
    C. carrying out your duty of enforcing the regulation as well as you can without com-
        ment
    D. suggesting to your clients that you may overlook violations of the regulation

12. One of the observations made in a recent psychological study of leadership is that the   12._____
    behavior of a new employee in a leadership position can be predicted more accurately on
    the basis of the behavior of the previous incumbent in the post than on the behavior of
    the new employee in his previous job.
    The BEST explanation for this observation is that there is a tendency

    A. for a newly appointed executive to avoid making basic changes in operational pro-
        cedures
    B. to choose similar types of personalities to fill the same type of position
    C. for a given organizational structure and set of duties and responsibilities to produce
        similar patterns of behavior
    D. for executives to develop more mature patterns of behavior as a result of increased
        responsibility

13. A director finds that reports submitted to him by his subordinates tend to emphasize the   13._____
    favorable and minimize the unfavorable aspects of situations.
    The MOST valid reason for this is that

    A. subordinates usually hesitate to give their supervisors an honest picture of a situa-
        tion
    B. the director may not have been sufficiently critical of previous reports submitted by
        his subordinates
    C. subordinates have a normal tendency to represent themselves and their actions in
        the best possible light
    D. many subordinates in the field have developed a tendency to understatement in
        the depiction of unfavorable situations

14. Effective delegation of authority and responsibility to subordinates is essential for the   14._____
    proper administration of a center. However, the director should retain some activities
    under his direct control.
    Of the following activities, the one for which there is LEAST justification for delegation
    by the director to a subordinate is one involving

    A. relationships with client groups
    B. physical danger to clients
    C. policies which are unpopular with staff
    D. matters for which there are no established policies

15. According to the principle of *span of control,* there should be a limited number of subordi-   15._____
    nates reporting to one supervisor.
    Of the following, the CHIEF disadvantage which may result from the application of this
    principle is a reduction in the

   A. contact between lower ranking staff members and higher ranking administrative personnel
   B. freedom of action of subordinates
   C. authority and responsibility of subordinates
   D. number of organizational levels through which a matter must pass before action is taken

16. The CHIEF objection to a practice of decentralizing the preparation and distribution of memoranda by bureaus, rather than controlling distribution through central office, is that it is LIKELY to result in   16.____

   A. overloading bureaus with a multiplicity of communications
   B. limited and specialized rather than broad and general viewpoints in the memoranda
   C. violation of the principle of unity of command
   D. unimportant information being communicated to all bureaus

17. A report has been completed by members of your staff. As director, you have reviewed the report and feel that the information revealed could be damaging to the department. You find yourself in conflict in your multiple role as director, as a professional, and as a citizen.
The one of the following actions which would be MOST desirable for you to take FIRST would be to   17.____

   A. send a copy of the report to your supervisor and request an immediate conference with him
   B. instruct staff to re-check the report and defer issuance of the report until the findings are confirmed
   C. immediately share the report with your supervisors and your advisory committee
   D. file the report until your advisory committee makes a request for it

18. In order for employees to function effectively, they should have a feeling of being treated fairly by management. Which of the following general policies is MOST likely to give employees such a feeling?   18.____

   A. An employee publication should be mailed directly to the home of each employee.
   B. Employee attitude surveys should be conducted at regular intervals.
   C. Employees should be consulted and kept informed on all matters that affect them.
   D. Employees should be informed when the press publishes statements of policy.

19. In order to give employees greater job satisfaction, some management experts advocate a policy of job enrichment. The one of the following which would be the BEST example of job enrichment is to   19.____

   A. allow an aide to decide which portion of his normal duties and responsibilities he prefers
   B. increase the fringe benefits currently available to paraprofessional employees
   C. add variety to the duties of an employee
   D. permit more flexible working schedules for professional employees

20. Management of large organizations has often emphasized high salaries and fringe bene-   20.____
fits as the most important means of motivating employees.
The one of the following which is NOT an argument used to support this approach is

    A. most people endure work mainly in order to collect the rewards and to have the opportunity to enjoy them
    B. material incentives have proved to be the best means of stimulating creative capacity and the will to work
    C. the majority of employees place little emphasis on work-centered motivation to perform
    D. numerous research studies have shown that pay ranks first on a scale of factors motivating employees in government and industry in the United States

21. Some organizations provide psychologists or other professionally trained persons with   21.____
whom employees can consult on a confidential basis regarding personal problems. Of
the following, which is MOST likely to be a benefit management can derive from such a
practice?

    A. Increase in the authority of management
    B. Disclosure of the corrupt practices of those handling money
    C. Receipt of new ideas and approaches to organizational problems
    D. Obtaining tighter control on employees' private behavior

22. Authorities agree that it is generally most desirable for an employee experiencing mental   22.____
health problems to seek competent professional help without being required or forced to
do so by another person.
They view self-referral as a most desirable action PRIMARILY because

    A. it shows that the employee probably is more aware of the problem and more highly motivated to solve his problems
    B. the employee's right to privacy in his personal affairs is maintained
    C. another person cannot be blamed in the event the outcome of the referral is not successful
    D. the employee knows best his problems and will do what is necessary to serve his own best interests

Questions 23-25.

DIRECTIONS: Questions 23 through 25 consist of three excerpts each. Consider an excerpt correct if all the statements in the excerpt are correct. Mark your answer as follows:

        A. if only excerpts 1 and 2 are correct
        B. if only excerpts 2 and 3 are correct
        C. if only excerpt 1 is correct
        D. if only excerpt 2 is correct

23. 1. Many executive decisions are based on assumptions.   23.____
They may be assumptions supported by sketchy data about future needs for services; assumptions about the attitudes and future behavior of employees, perhaps based on reports of staff members or hearsay evidence; or assumptions about agency values that are as much a reflection of personal desires as of agency goals.
    2. A good pattern of well-conceived plans is only a first step in administration. The administrator must also create an organization to formulate and carry out such plans. Resources must be assembled; supervision of actual operations is necessary; and before the executive's task is completed, he must exercise control.
    3. When a problem is well defined, good alternatives identified, and the likely consequences of each alternative forecast as best we can, one can assume that the final choice of action to be taken would be easy, if not obvious.

24. 1. Principles of motivation are not difficult to establish because human behavior is not   24.____
complex and is easily understood; individual differences in human beings are substantial; and people are continuously learning and changing.
    2. What gives employees satisfaction or dissatisfaction indicates the nature of the motivation problem and provides positive guidance to the administrator who faces the problem of trying to get people to carry out a set of plans.
    3. The administrator's job of motivation can be described as that of creating a situation in which actions that provide net satisfaction to individual members of the enterprise are at the same time actions that make appropriate contributions toward the objectives of the enterprise.

25. 1. Administrative organization is primarily concerned with legal, technical, or ultimate   25.____
authority; the operational authority relationships that may be created by organization are of major significance.
    2. Accountability is not removed by delegation. Appraisal of results should be tempered by the extent to which an administrator must rely on subordinates.
    3. In delegations to operating subordinates, authority to plan exceeds authority to do, inasmuch as the executive typically reserves some of the planning for himself.

KEY (CORRECT ANSWERS)

1.	C		11.	B
2.	A		12.	C
3.	B		13.	C
4.	B		14.	D
5.	B		15.	A
6.	C		16.	A
7.	A		17.	B
8.	B		18.	C
9.	C		19.	C
10.	D		20.	D

21.	C
22.	A
23.	A
24.	B
25.	D

PHILOSOPHY, PRINCIPLES, PRACTICES AND TECHNICS
OF
SUPERVISION, ADMINISTRATION, MANAGEMENT AND ORGANIZATION

TABLE OF CONTENTS

TABLE OF CONTENTS (CONTINUED)

PHILOSOPHY, PRINCIPLES, PRACTICES, AND TECHNICS
OF
SUPERVISION, ADMINISTRATION, MANAGEMENT AND ORGANIZATION

I. MEANING OF SUPERVISION

The extension of the democratic philosophy has been accompanied by an extension in the scope of supervision. Modern leaders and supervisors no longer think of supervision in the narrow sense of being confined chiefly to visiting employees, supplying materials, or rating the staff. They regard supervision as being intimately related to all the concerned agencies of society, they speak of the supervisor's function in terms of "growth", rather than the "improvement," of employees.

This modern concept of supervision may be defined as follows:

Supervision is leadership and the development of leadership within groups which are cooperatively engaged in inspection, research, training, guidance and evaluation.

II. THE OLD AND THE NEW SUPERVISION

TRADITIONAL
1. Inspection
2. Focused on the employee
3. Visitation
4. Random and haphazard
5. Imposed and authoritarian
6. One person usually

MODERN
1. Study and analysis
2. Focused on aims, materials, methods, supervisors, employees, environment
3. Demonstrations, intervisitation, workshops, directed reading, bulletins, etc.
4. Definitely organized and planned (scientific)
5. Cooperative and democratic
6. Many persons involved (creative)

III THE EIGHT (8) BASIC PRINCIPLES OF THE NEW SUPERVISION

1. *PRINCIPLE OF RESPONSIBILITY*
Authority to act and responsibility for acting must be joined.
   a. If you give responsibility, give authority.
   b. Define employee duties clearly.
   c. Protect employees from criticism by others.
   d. Recognize the rights as well as obligations of employees.
   e. Achieve the aims of a democratic society insofar as it is possible within the area of your work.
   f. Establish a situation favorable to training and learning.
   g. Accept ultimate responsibility for everything done in your section, unit, office, division, department.
   h. Good administration and good supervision are inseparable.

2. *PRINCIPLE OF AUTHORITY*

The success of the supervisor is measured by the extent to which the power of authority is not used.

    a. Exercise simplicity and informality in supervision.
    b. Use the simplest machinery of supervision.
    c. If it is good for the organization as a whole, it is probably justified.
    d. Seldom be arbitrary or authoritative.
    e. Do not base your work on the power of position or of personality.
    f. Permit and encourage the free expression of opinions.

3. *PRINCIPLE OF SELF-GROWTH*

The success of the supervisor is measured by the extent to which, and the speed with which, he is no longer needed.

    a. Base criticism on principles, not on specifics.
    b. Point out higher activities to employees.
    c. Train for self-thinking by employees, to meet new situations.
    d. Stimulate initiative, self-reliance and individual responsibility.
    e. Concentrate on stimulating the growth of employees rather than on removing defects.

4. *PRINCIPLE OF INDIVIDUAL WORTH*

Respect for the individual is a paramount consideration in supervision.

    a. Be human and sympathetic in dealing with employees.
    b. Don't nag about things to be done.
    c. Recognize the individual differences among employees and seek opportunities to permit best expression of each personality.

5. *PRINCIPLE OF CREATIVE LEADERSHIP*

The best supervision is that which is not apparent to the employee.

    a. Stimulate, don't drive employees to creative action.
    b. Emphasize doing good things.
    c. Encourage employees to do what they do best.
    d. Do not be too greatly concerned with details of subject or method.
    e. Do not be concerned exclusively with immediate problems and activities.
    f. Reveal higher activities and make them both desired and maximally possible.
    g. Determine procedures in the light of each situation but see that these are derived from a sound basic philosophy.
    h. Aid, inspire and lead so as to liberate the creative spirit latent in all good employees.

6. *PRINCIPLE OF SUCCESS AND FAILURE*

There are no unsuccessful employees, only unsuccessful supervisors who have failed to give proper leadership.

    a. Adapt suggestions to the capacities, attitudes, and prejudices of employees.
    b. Be gradual, be progressive, be persistent.
    c. Help the employee find the general principle; have the employee apply his own problem to the general principle.
    d. Give adequate appreciation for good work and honest effort.
    e. Anticipate employee difficulties and help to prevent them.
    f. Encourage employees to do the desirable things they will do anyway.
    g. Judge your supervision by the results it secures.

7. *PRINCIPLE OF SCIENCE*
Successful supervision is scientific, objective, and experimental. It is based on facts, not on prejudices.
        a. Be cumulative in results.
        b. Never divorce your suggestions from the goals of training.
        c. Don't be impatient of results.
        d. Keep all matters on a professional, not a personal level.
        e. Do not be concerned exclusively with immediate problems and activities.
        f. Use objective means of determining achievement and rating where possible.

8. *PRINCIPLE OF COOPERATION*
Supervision is a cooperative enterprise between supervisor and employee.
        a. Begin with conditions as they are.
        b. Ask opinions of all involved when formulating policies.
        c. Organization is as good as its weakest link.
        d. Let employees help to determine policies and department programs.
        e. Be approachable and accessible - physically and mentally.
        f. Develop pleasant social relationships.

IV. WHAT IS ADMINISTRATION?

Administration is concerned with providing the environment, the material facilities, and the operational procedures that will promote the maximum growth and development of supervisors and employees. (Organization is an aspect, and a concomitant, of administration.)

There is no sharp line of demarcation between supervision and administration; these functions are intimately interrelated and, often, overlapping. They are complementary activities.

1. *PRACTICES COMMONLY CLASSED AS "SUPERVISORY"*
        a. Conducting employees conferences
        b. Visiting sections, units, offices, divisions, departments
        c. Arranging for demonstrations
        d. Examining plans
        e. Suggesting professional reading
        f. Interpreting bulletins
        g. Recommending in-service training courses
        h. Encouraging experimentation
        i. Appraising employee morale
        j. Providing for intervisitation

2. *PRACTICES COMMONLY CLASSIFIED AS "ADMINISTRATIVE"*
        a. Management of the office
        b. Arrangement of schedules for extra duties
        c. Assignment of rooms or areas
        d. Distribution of supplies
        e. Keeping records and reports
        f. Care of audio-visual materials
        g. Keeping inventory records
        h. Checking record cards and books
        i. Programming special activities
        j. Checking on the attendance and punctuality of employees

3. *PRACTICES COMMONLY CLASSIFIED AS BOTH "SUPERVISORY" AND "ADMINISTRATIVE"*
   a. Program construction
   b. Testing or evaluating outcomes
   c. Personnel accounting
   d. Ordering instructional materials

V. RESPONSIBILITIES OF THE SUPERVISOR

A person employed in a supervisory capacity must constantly be able to improve his own efficiency and ability. He represents the employer to the employees and only continuous self-examination can make him a capable supervisor.

Leadership and training are the supervisor's responsibility. An efficient working unit is one in which the employees work with the supervisor. It is his job to bring out the best in his employees. He must always be relaxed, courteous and calm in his association with his employees. Their feelings are important, and a harsh attitude does not develop the most efficient employees.

VI. COMPETENCIES OF THE SUPERVISOR

1. Complete knowledge of the duties and responsibilities of his position.
2. To be able to organize a job, plan ahead and carry through.
3. To have self-confidence and initiative.
4. To be able to handle the unexpected situation and make quick decisions.
5. To be able to properly train subordinates in the positions they are best suited for.
6. To be able to keep good human relations among his subordinates.
7. To be able to keep good human relations between his subordinates and himself and to earn their respect and trust.

VII. THE PROFESSIONAL SUPERVISOR-EMPLOYEE RELATIONSHIP

There are two kinds of efficiency: one kind is only apparent and is produced in organizations through the exercise of mere discipline; this is but a simulation of the second, or true, efficiency which springs from spontaneous cooperation. If you are a manager, no matter how great or small your responsibility, it is your job, in the final analysis, to create and develop this involuntary cooperation among the people whom you supervise. For, no matter how powerful a combination of money, machines, and materials a company may have, this is a dead and sterile thing without a team of willing, thinking and articulate people to guide it.

The following 21 points are presented as indicative of the exemplary basic relationship that should exist between supervisor and employee:

1. Each person wants to be liked and respected by his fellow employee and wants to be treated with consideration and respect by his superior.
2. The most competent employee will make an error. However, in a unit where good relations exist between the supervisor and his employees, tenseness and fear do not exist. Thus, errors are not hidden or covered up and the efficiency of a unit is not impaired.
3. Subordinates resent rules, regulations, or orders that are unreasonable or unexplained.
4. Subordinates are quick to resent unfairness, harshness, injustices and favoritism.
5. An employee will accept responsibility if he knows that he will be complimented for a job well done, and not too harshly chastised for failure; that his supervisor will check the cause of the failure, and, if it was the supervisor's fault, he will assume the blame therefore. If it was the employee's fault, his supervisor will explain the correct method or means of handling the responsibility.

6. An employee wants to receive credit for a suggestion he has made, that is used. If a suggestion cannot be used, the employee is entitled to an explanation. The supervisor should not say "no" and close the subject.
7. Fear and worry slow up a worker's ability. Poor working environment can impair his physical and mental health. A good supervisor avoids forceful methods, threats and arguments to get a job done.
8. A forceful supervisor is able to train his employees individually and as a team, and is able to motivate them in the proper channels.
9. A mature supervisor is able to properly evaluate his subordinates and to keep them happy and satisfied.
10. A sensitive supervisor will never patronize his subordinates.
11. A worthy supervisor will respect his employees' confidences.
12. Definite and clear-cut responsibilities should be assigned to each executive.
13. Responsibility should always be coupled with corresponding authority.
14. No change should be made in the scope or responsibilities of a position without a definite understanding to that effect on the part of all persons concerned.
15. No executive or employee, occupying a single position in the organization, should be subject to definite orders from more than one source.
16. Orders should never be given to subordinates over the head of a responsible executive. Rather than do this, the officer in question should be supplanted.
17. Criticisms of subordinates should, whoever possible, be made privately, and in no case should a subordinate be criticized in the presence of executives or employees of equal or lower rank.
18. No dispute or difference between executives or employees as to authority or responsibilities should be considered too trivial for prompt and careful adjudication.
19. Promotions, wage changes, and disciplinary action should always be approved by the executive immediately superior to the one directly responsible.
20. No executive or employee should ever be required, or expected, to be at the same time an assistant to, and critic of, another.
21. Any executive whose work is subject to regular inspection should, whever practicable, be given the assistance and facilities necessary to enable him to maintain an independent check of the quality of his work.

VIII. MINI-TEXT IN SUPERVISION, ADMINISTRATION, MANAGEMENT, AND ORGANIZATION

A. BRIEF HIGHLIGHTS

Listed concisely and sequentially are major headings and important data in the field for quick recall and review.

1. *LEVELS OF MANAGEMENT*
Any organization of some size has several levels of management. In terms of a ladder the levels are:

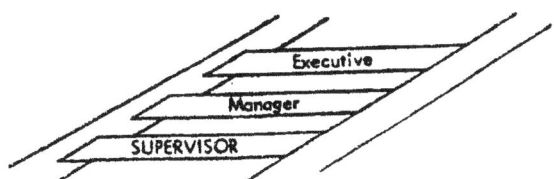

The first level is very important because it is the beginning point of management leadership.

2. *WHAT THE SUPERVISOR MUST LEARN*

A supervisor must learn to:
(1) Deal with people and their differences
(2) Get the job done through people
(3) Recognize the problems when they exist
(4) Overcome obstacles to good performance
(5) Evaluate the performance of people
(6) Check his own performance in terms of accomplishment

3. *A DEFINITION OF SUPERVISOR*

The term supervisor means any individual having authority, in the interests of the employer, to hire, transfer, suspend, lay-off, recall, promote, discharge, assign, reward, or discipline other employees or responsibility to direct them, or to adjust their grievances, or effectively to recommend such action, if, in connection with the foregoing, exercise of such authority is not of a merely routine or clerical nature but requires the use of independent judgment.

4. *ELEMENTS OF THE TEAM CONCEPT*

What is involved in teamwork? The component parts are:

(1) Members	(3) Goals	(5) Cooperation
(2) A leader	(4) Plans	(6) Spirit

5. *PRINCIPLES OF ORGANIZATION*

(1) A team member must know what his job is.
(2) Be sure that the nature and scope of a job are understood.
(3) Authority and responsibility should be carefully spelled out.
(4) A supervisor should be permitted to make the maximum number of decisions affecting his employees.
(5) Employees should report to only one supervisor.
(6) A supervisor should direct only as many employees as he can handle effectively.
(7) An organization plan should be flexible.
(8) Inspection and performance of work should be separate.
(9) Organizational problems should receive immediate attention.
(10) Assign work in line with ability and experience.

6. *THE FOUR IMPORTANT PARTS OF EVERY JOB*

(1) Inherent in every job is the *accountability* for results.
(2) A second set of factors in every job is *responsibilities.*
(3) Along with duties and responsibilities one must have the *authority* to act within certain limits without obtaining permission to proceed.
(4) No job exists in a vacuum. The supervisor is surrounded by key *relationships.*

7. *PRINCIPLES OF DELEGATION*

Where work is delegated for the first time, the supervisor should think in terms of these questions:
(1) Who is best qualified to do this?
(2) Can an employee improve his abilities by doing this?
(3) How long should an employee spend on this?
(4) Are there any special problems for which he will need guidance?
(5) How broad a delegation can I make?

8. PRINCIPLES OF EFFECTIVE COMMUNICATIONS
    (1) Determine the media
    (2) To whom directed?
    (3) Identification and source authority
    (4) Is communication understood?

9. PRINCIPLES OF WORK IMPROVEMENT
    (1) Most people usually do only the work which is assigned to them
    (2) Workers are likely to fit assigned work into the time available to perform it
    (3) A good workload usually stimulates output
    (4) People usually do their best work when they know that results will be reviewed or inspected
    (5) Employees usually feel that someone else is responsible for conditions of work, workplace layout, job methods, type of tools/equipment, and other such factors
    (6) Employees are usually defensive about their job security
    (7) Employees have natural resistance to change
    (8) Employees can support or destroy a supervisor
    (9) A supervisor usually earns the respect of his people through his personal example of diligence and efficiency

10. AREAS OF JOB IMPROVEMENT
The areas of job improvement are quite numerous, but the most common ones which a supervisor can identify and utilize are:

(1) Departmental layout	(5) Work methods
(2) Flow of work	(6) Materials handling
(3) Workplace layout	(7) Utilization
(4) Utilization of manpower	(8) Motion economy

11. SEVEN KEY POINTS IN MAKING IMPROVEMENTS
    (1) Select the job to be improved
    (2) Study how it is being done now
    (3) Question the present method
    (4) Determine actions to be taken
    (5) Chart proposed method
    (6) Get approval and apply
    (7) Solicit worker participation

12. CORRECTIVE TECHNIQUES OF JOB IMPROVEMENT

Specific Problems	General Improvement	Corrective Techniques
(1) Size of workload	(1) Departmental layout	(1) Study with scale model
(2) Inability to meet schedules	(2) Flow of work	(2) Flow chart study
(3) Strain and fatigue	(3) Work plan layout	(3) Motion analysis
(4) Improper use of men and skills	(4) Utilization of manpower	(4) Comparison of units produced to standard allowance
(5) Waste, poor quality, unsafe conditions	(5) Work methods	(5) Methods analysis
(6) Bottleneck conditions that hinder output	(6) Materials handling	(6) Flow chart & equipment study
(7) Poor utilization of equipment and machine	(7) Utilization of equipment	(7) Down time vs. running time
(8) Efficiency and productivity of labor	(8) Motion economy	(8) Motion analysis

13. A *PLANNING CHECKLIST*

(1) Objectives	(6) Resources	(11) Safety
(2) Controls	(7) Manpower	(12) Money
(3) Delegations	(8) Equipment	(13) Work
(4) Communications	(9) Supplies and materials	(14) Timing of improvements
(5) Resources	(10) Utilization of time	

14. *FIVE CHARACTERISTICS OF GOOD DIRECTIONS*

In order to get results, directions must be:

(1) Possible of accomplishment	(3) Related to mission	(5) Unmistakably clear
(2) Agreeable with worker interests	(4) Planned and complete	

15. *TYPES OF DIRECTIONS*

(1) Demands or direct orders	(3) Suggestion or implication
(2) Requests	(4) Volunteering

16. *CONTROLS*

A typical listing of the overall areas in which the supervisor should establish controls might be:

(1) Manpower	(3) Quality of work	(5) Time	(7) Money
(2) Materials	(4) Quantity of work	(6) Space	(8) Methods

17. *ORIENTING THE NEW EMPLOYEE*

(1) Prepare for him	(3) Orientation for the job
(2) Welcome the new employee	(4) Follow-up

18. *CHECKLIST FOR ORIENTING NEW EMPLOYEES*

	Yes	No
(1) Do your appreciate the feelings of new employees when they first report for work?	____	____
(2) Are you aware of the fact that the new employee must make a big adjustment to his job?	____	____
(3) Have you given him good reasons for liking the job and the organization?	____	____
(4) Have you prepared for his first day on the job?		
(5) Did you welcome him cordially and make him feel needed?		
(6) Did you establish rapport with him so that he feels free to talk and discuss matters with you?	____	____
(7) Did you explain his job to him and his relationship to you?	____	____
(8) Does he know that his work will be evaluated periodically on a basis that is fair and objective?	____	____
(9) Did you introduce him to his fellow workers in such a way that they are likely to accept him?	____	____
(10) Does he know what employee benefits he will receive?		
(11) Does he understand the importance of being on the job and what to do if he must leave his duty station?	____	____
(12) Has he been impressed with the importance of accident prevention and safe practice?	____	____
(13) Does he generally know his way around the department?	____	____
(14) Is he under the guidance of a sponsor who will teach the right ways of doing things?	____	____
(15) Do you plan to follow-up so that he will continue to adjust successfully to his job?	____	____

19. *PRINCIPLES OF LEARNING*
    (1) Motivation   (2) Demonstration or explanation   (3) Practice

20. *CAUSES OF POOR PERFORMANCE*
    (1) Improper training for job
    (2) Wrong tools
    (3) Inadequate directions
    (4) Lack of supervisory follow-up
    (5) Poor communications
    (6) Lack of standards of performance
    (7) Wrong work habits
    (8) Low morale
    (9) Other

21. *FOUR MAJOR STEPS IN ON-THE-JOB INSTRUCTION*
    (1) Prepare the worker
    (2) Present the operation
    (3) Tryout performance
    (4) Follow-up

22. *EMPLOYEES WANT FIVE THINGS*
    (1) Security (2) Opportunity (3) Recognition (4) Inclusion (5) Expression

23. *SOME DON'TS IN REGARD TO PRAISE*
    (1) Don't praise a person for something he hasn't done
    (2) Don't praise a person unless you can be sincere
    (3) Don't be sparing in praise just because your superior withholds it from you
    (4) Don't let too much time elapse between good performance and recognition of it

24. *HOW TO GAIN YOUR WORKERS' CONFIDENCE*
Methods of developing confidence include such things as:
    (1) Knowing the interests, habits, hobbies of employees
    (2) Admitting your own inadequacies
    (3) Sharing and telling of confidence in others
    (4) Supporting people when they are in trouble
    (5) Delegating matters that can be well handled
    (6) Being frank and straightforward about problems and working conditions
    (7) Encouraging others to bring their problems to you
    (8) Taking action on problems which impede worker progress

25. *SOURCES OF EMPLOYEE PROBLEMS*
On-the-job causes might be such things as:
    (1) A feeling that favoritism is exercised in assignments
    (2) Assignment of overtime
    (3) An undue amount of supervision
    (4) Changing methods or systems
    (5) Stealing of ideas or trade secrets
    (6) Lack of interest in job
    (7) Threat of reduction in force
    (8) Ignorance or lack of communications
    (9) Poor equipment
    (10) Lack of knowing how supervisor feels toward employee
    (11) Shift assignments

Off-the-job problems might have to do with:
    (1) Health   (2) Finances   (3) Housing   (4) Family

26. THE SUPERVISOR'S KEY TO DISCIPLINE

There are several key points about discipline which the supervisor should keep in mind:
(1) Job discipline is one of the disciplines of life and is directed by the supervisor.
(2) It is more important to correct an employee fault than to fix blame for it.
(3) Employee performance is affected by problems both on the job and off.
(4) Sudden or abrupt changes in behavior can be indications of important employee problems.
(5) Problems should be dealt with as soon as possible after they are identified.
(6) The attitude of the supervisor may have more to do with solving problems than the techniques of problem solving.
(7) Correction of employee behavior should be resorted to only after the supervisor is sure that training or counseling will not be helpful.
(8) Be sure to document your disciplinary actions.
(9) Make sure that you are disciplining on the basis of facts rather than personal feelings.
(10) Take each disciplinary step in order, being careful not to make snap judgments, or decisions based on impatience.

27. FIVE IMPORTANT PROCESSES OF MANAGEMENT

(1) Planning (2) Organizing (3) Scheduling
(4) Controlling (5) Motivating

28. WHEN THE SUPERVISOR FAILS TO PLAN

(1) Supervisor creates impression of not knowing his job
(2) May lead to excessive overtime
(3) Job runs itself -- supervisor lacks control
(4) Deadlines and appointments missed
(5) Parts of the work go undone
(6) Work interrupted by emergencies
(7) Sets a bad example
(8) Uneven workload creates peaks and valleys
(9) Too much time on minor details at expense of more important tasks

29. FOURTEEN GENERAL PRINCIPLES OF MANAGEMENT

(1) Division of work
(2) Authority and responsibility
(3) Discipline
(4) Unity of command
(5) Unity of direction
(6) Subordination of individual interest to general interest
(7) Remuneration of personnel
(8) Centralization
(9) Scalar chain
(10) Order
(11) Equity
(12) Stability of tenure of personnel
(13) Initiative
(14) Esprit de corps

30. CHANGE

Bringing about change is perhaps attempted more often, and yet less well understood, than anything else the supervisor does. How do people generally react to change? (People tend to resist change that is imposed upon them by other individuals or circumstances.

Change is characteristic of every situation. It is a part of every real endeavor where the efforts of people are concerned.

A. Why do people resist change?
People may resist change because of:
(1) Fear of the unknown
(2) Implied criticism
(3) Unpleasant experiences in the past
(4) Fear of loss of status
(5) Threat to the ego
(6) Fear of loss of economic stability

B. How can we best overcome the resistance to change?
In initiating change, take these steps:
(1) Get ready to sell
(2) Identify sources of help
(3) Anticipate objections
(4) Sell benefits
(5) Listen in depth
(6) Follow up

B. BRIEF TOPICAL SUMMARIES

I. WHO/WHAT IS THE SUPERVISOR?
1. The supervisor is often called the "highest level employee and the lowest level manager."
2. A supervisor is a member of both management and the work group. He acts as a bridge between the two.
3. Most problems in supervision are in the area of human relations, or people problems.
4. Employees expect: Respect, opportunity to learn and to advance, and a sense of belonging, and so forth.
5. Supervisors are responsible for directing people and organizing work. Planning is of paramount importance.
6. A position description is a set of duties and responsibilities inherent to a given position.
7. It is important to keep the position description up-to-date and to provide each employee with his own copy.

II. THE SOCIOLOGY OF WORK
1. People are alike in many ways; however, each individual is unique.
2. The supervisor is challenged in getting to know employee differences. Acquiring skills in evaluating individuals is an asset.
3. Maintaining meaningful working relationships in the organization is of great importance.
4. The supervisor has an obligation to help individuals to develop to their fullest potential.
5. Job rotation on a planned basis helps to build versatility and to maintain interest and enthusiasm in work groups.
6. Cross training (job rotation) provides backup skills.
7. The supervisor can help reduce tension by maintaining a sense of humor, providing guidance to employees, and by making reasonable and timely decisions. Employees respond favorably to working under reasonably predictable circumstances.
8. Change is characteristic of all managerial behavior. The supervisor must adjust to changes in procedures, new methods, technological changes, and to a number of new and sometimes challenging situations.
9. To overcome the natural tendency for people to resist change, the supervisor should become more skillful in initiating change.

III. PRINCIPLES AND PRACTICES OF SUPERVISION

1. Employees should be required to answer to only one superior.
2. A supervisor can effectively direct only a limited number of employees, depending upon the complexity, variety, and proximity of the jobs involved.
3. The organizational chart presents the organization in graphic form. It reflects lines of authority and responsibility as well as interrelationships of units within the organization.
4. Distribution of work can be improved through an analysis using the "Work Distribution Chart."
5. The "Work Distribution Chart" reflects the division of work within a unit in understandable form.
6. When related tasks are given to an employee, he has a better chance of increasing his skills through training.
7. The individual who is given the responsibility for tasks must also be given the appropriate authority to insure adequate results.
8. The supervisor should delegate repetitive, routine work. Preparation of recurring reports, maintaining leave and attendance records are some examples.
9. Good discipline is essential to good task performance. Discipline is reflected in the actions of employees on the job in the absence of supervision.
10. Disciplinary action may have to be taken when the positive aspects of discipline have failed. Reprimand, warning, and suspension are examples of disciplinary action.
11. If a situation calls for a reprimand, be sure it is deserved and remember it is to be done in private.

IV. DYNAMIC LEADERSHIP

1. A style is a personal method or manner of exerting influence.
2. Authoritarian leaders often see themselves as the source of power and authority.
3. The democratic leader often perceives the group as the source of authority and power.
4. Supervisors tend to do better when using the pattern of leadership that is most natural for them.
5. Social scientists suggest that the effective supervisor use the leadership style that best fits the problem or circumstances involved.
6. All four styles -- telling, selling, consulting, joining -- have their place. Using one does not preclude using the other at another time.
7. The theory X point of view assumes that the average person dislikes work, will avoid it whenever possible, and must be coerced to achieve organizational objectives.
8. The theory Y point of view assumes that the average person considers work to be as natural as play, and, when the individual is committed, he requires little supervision or direction to accomplish desired objectives.
9. The leader's basic assumptions concerning human behavior and human nature affect his actions, decisions, and other managerial practices.
10. Dissatisfaction among employees is often present, but difficult to isolate. The supervisor should seek to weaken dissatisfaction by keeping promises, being sincere and considerate, keeping employees informed, and so forth.
11. Constructive suggestions should be encouraged during the natural progress of the work.

V. PROCESSES FOR SOLVING PROBLEMS

1. People find their daily tasks more meaningful and satisfying when they can improve them.
2. The causes of problems, or the key factors, are often hidden in the background. Ability to solve problems often involves the ability to isolate them from their backgrounds. There is some substance to the cliché that some persons "can't see the forest for the trees."
3. New procedures are often developed from old ones. Problems should be broken down into manageable parts. New ideas can be adapted from old ones.

4. People think differently in problem-solving situations. Using a logical, patterned approach is often useful. One approach found to be useful includes these steps:
   - (a) Define the problem
   - (b) Establish objectives
   - (c) Get the facts
   - (d) Weigh and decide
   - (e) Take action
   - (f) Evaluate action

VI. TRAINING FOR RESULTS
1. Participants respond best when they feel training is important to them.
2. The supervisor has responsibility for the training and development of those who report to him.
3. When training is delegated to others, great care must be exercised to insure the trainer has knowledge, aptitude, and interest for his work as a trainer.
4. Training (learning) of some type goes on continually. The most successful supervisor makes certain the learning contributes in a productive manner to operational goals.
5. New employees are particularly susceptible to training. Older employees facing new job situations require specific training, as well as having need for development and growth opportunities.
6. Training needs require continuous monitoring.
7. The training officer of an agency is a professional with a responsibility to assist supervisors in solving training problems.
8. Many of the self-development steps important to the supervisor's own growth are equally important to the development of peers and subordinates. Knowledge of these is important when the supervisor consults with others on development and growth opportunities.

VII. HEALTH, SAFETY, AND ACCIDENT PREVENTION
1. Management-minded supervisors take appropriate measures to assist employees in maintaining health and in assuring safe practices in the work environment.
2. Effective safety training and practices help to avoid injury and accidents.
3. Safety should be a management goal. All infractions of safety which are observed should be corrected without exception.
4. Employees' safety attitude, training and instruction, provision of safe tools and equipment, supervision, and leadership are considered highly important factors which contribute to safety and which can be influenced directly by supervisors.
5. When accidents do occur they should be investigated promptly for very important reasons, including the fact that information which is gained can be used to prevent accidents in the future.

VIII. EQUAL EMPLOYMENT OPPORTUNITY
1. The supervisor should endeavor to treat all employees fairly, without regard to religion, race, sex, or national origin.
2. Groups tend to reflect the attitude of the leader. Prejudice can be detected even in very subtle form. Supervisors must strive to create a feeling of mutual respect and confidence in every employee.
3. Complete utilization of all human resources is a national goal. Equitable consideration should be accorded women in the work force, minority-group members, the physically and mentally handicapped, and the older employee. The important question is: "Who can do the job?"
4. Training opportunities, recognition for performance, overtime assignments, promotional opportunities, and all other personnel actions are to be handled on an equitable basis.

- 14 -

IX. IMPROVING COMMUNICATIONS

1. Communications is achieving understanding between the sender and the receiver of a message. It also means sharing information -- the creation of understanding.
2. Communication is basic to all human activity. Words are means of conveying meanings; however, real meanings are in people.
3. There are very practical differences in the effectiveness of one-way, impersonal, and two-way communications. Words spoken face-to-face are better understood. Telephone conversations are effective, but lack the rapport of person-to-person exchanges. The whole person communicates.
4. Cooperation and communication in an organization go hand in hand. When there is a mutual respect between people, spelling out rules and procedures for communicating is unnecessary.
5. There are several barriers to effective communications. These include failure to listen with respect and understanding, lack of skill in feedback, and misinterpreting the meanings of words used by the speaker. It is also common practice to listen to what we want to hear, and tune out things we do not want to hear.
6. Communication is management's chief problem. The supervisor should accept the challenge to communicate more effectively and to improve interagency and intra-agency communications.
7. The supervisor may often plan for and conduct meetings. The planning phase is critical and may determine the success or the failure of a meeting.
8. Speaking before groups usually requires extra effort. Stage fright may never disappear completely, but it can be controlled.

X. SELF-DEVELOPMENT

1. Every employee is responsible for his own self-development.
2. Toastmaster and toastmistress clubs offer opportunities to improve skills in oral communications.
3. Planning for one's own self-development is of vital importance. Supervisors know their own strengths and limitations better than anyone else.
4. Many opportunities are open to aid the supervisor in his developmental efforts, including job assignments; training opportunities, both governmental and non-governmental -- to include universities and professional conferences and seminars.
5. Programmed instruction offers a means of studying at one's own rate.
6. Where difficulties may arise from a supervisor's being away from his work for training, he may participate in televised home study or correspondence courses to meet his self-develop- ment needs.

XI. TEACHING AND TRAINING

A. The Teaching Process

Teaching is encouraging and guiding the learning activities of students toward established goals. In most cases this process consists in five steps: preparation, presentation, summarization, evaluation, and application.

1. Preparation

Preparation is twofold in nature; that of the supervisor and the employee.
Preparation by the supervisor is absolutely essential to success. He must know what, when, where, how, and whom he will teach. Some of the factors that should be considered are:

(1) The objectives
(2) The materials needed
(3) The methods to be used
(4) Employee participation
(5) Employee interest
(6) Training aids
(7) Evaluation
(8) Summarization

134

Employee preparation consists in preparing the employee to receive the material. Probably the most important single factor in the preparation of the employee is arousing and maintaining his interest. He must know the objectives of the training, why he is there, how the material can be used, and its importance to him.

2. Presentation

In presentation, have a carefully designed plan and follow it.
The plan should be accurate and complete, yet flexible enough to meet situations as they arise. The method of presentation will be determined by the particular situation and objectives.

3. Summary

A summary should be made at the end of every training unit and program. In addition, there may be internal summaries depending on the nature of the material being taught. The important thing is that the trainee must always be able to understand how each part of the new material relates to the whole.

4. Application

The supervisor must arrange work so the employee will be given a chance to apply new knowledge or skills while the material is still clear in his mind and interest is high. The trainee does not really know whether he has learned the material until he has been given a chance to apply it. If the material is not applied, it loses most of its value.

5. Evaluation

The purpose of all training is to promote learning. To determine whether the training has been a success or failure, the supervisor must evaluate this learning.

In the broadest sense evaluation includes all the devices, methods, skills, and techniques used by the supervisor to keep him self and the employees informed as to their progress toward the objectives they are pursuing. The extent to which the employee has mastered the knowledge, skills, and abilities, or changed his attitudes, as determined by the program objectives, is the extent to which instruction has succeeded or failed.

Evaluation should not be confined to the end of the lesson, day, or program but should be used continuously. We shall note later the way this relates to the rest of the teaching process.

B. Teaching Methods

A teaching method is a pattern of identifiable student and instructor activity used in presenting training material.

All supervisors are faced with the problem of deciding which method should be used at a given time.

As with all methods, there are certain advantages and disadvantages to each method.

1. Lecture

The lecture is direct oral presentation of material by the supervisor. The present trend is to place less emphasis on the trainer's activity and more on that of the trainee.

2. Discussion

Teaching by discussion or conference involves using questions and other techniques to arouse interest and focus attention upon certain areas, and by doing so creating a learning situation. This can be one of the most valuable methods because it gives the employees 'an opportunity to express their ideas and pool their knowledge.

3. Demonstration

The demonstration is used to teach how something works or how to do something. It can be used to show a principle or what the results of a series of actions will be. A well-staged demonstration is particularly effective because it shows proper methods of performance in a realistic manner.

4. Performance

Performance is one of the most fundamental of all learning techniques or teaching methods. The trainee may be able to tell how a specific operation should be performed but he cannot be sure he knows how to perform the operation until he has done so.

5. Which Method to Use

Moreover, there are other methods and techniques of teaching. It is difficult to use any method without other methods entering into it. In any learning situation a combination of methods is usually more effective than anyone method alone.

Finally, evaluation must be integrated into the other aspects of the teaching-learning process.
It must be used in the motivation of the trainees; it must be used to assist in developing understanding during the training; and it must be related to employee application of the results of training.
This is distinctly the role of the supervisor.

CPSIA information can be obtained
at www.ICGtesting.com
Printed in the USA
BVHW011407020120
568385BV00009B/256/P